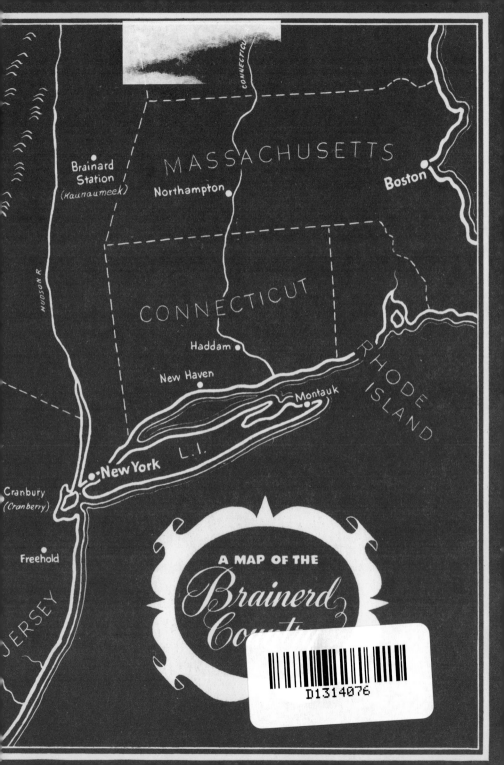

CONNECTICUT

MASSACHUSETTS

Brainard
Station
(Kaunaumeek)

Northampton

Boston

HUDSON R.

CONNECTICUT

Haddam

New Haven

RHODE ISLAND

Montauk

L. I.

New York

Cranbury
(Cranberry)

Freehold

JERSEY

A MAP OF THE

*Brainerd
Country*

Flagellant on Horseback

THE BROAD BRIM BOOKS

by

RICHARD ELLSWORTH DAY

THE SHADOW OF THE BROAD BRIM
(Life of Charles Haddon Spurgeon)

BUSH AGLOW
(Life of Dwight Lyman Moody)

BREAKFAST TABLE AUTOCRAT
(Life of Henry Parsons Crowell)

MAN OF LIKE PASSIONS
(Life of Charles Grandison Finney)

BEACON LIGHTS OF GRACE
(Twelve Biographical Vignettes)

THE BORROWED GLOW
(Daily Meditations)

FLAGELLANT ON HORSEBACK
(Life of David Brainerd)

RHAPSODY IN BLACK
(Life of John Jasper)
(In preparation)

Flagellant on Horseback

Horseback

The Life Story of
DAVID BRAINERD

by

RICHARD ELLSWORTH DAY

A BROAD BRIM BOOK

PHILADELPHIA
THE JUDSON PRESS

CHICAGO   LOS ANGELES

FLAGELLANT ON HORSEBACK

Copyright, 1950

By The Judson Press

First Edition

To

Mr. and Mrs. Egbert Wheeler Mersereau
of San Jose, California
who were among the first to esteem the Broad Brim
Books and who have remained the first in all the
years to encourage the writing of them, and

To

Henry Allan Ironside
whose words of commendation as
A Prince in Israel and Man of Letters
have filled me with a desire for excellence in
"this business of writing"

The Interpreter's House

"Before mounting for thy journey, pause at the Interpreter's House so that thou mayest understand." (John of Bedford)

* * *

The secret of Brainerd's exploits has been missed by his impulsive Boswells. For nearly two hundred years they have chanted, "It was his importunate prayer life." Not so! The hiding of his power was, to borrow an excellent Puritan phrase, "the mysterious constraint of Love Divine."

* * *

James M. Sherwood, in his *Memoirs of Revd. David Brainerd,* 1891, stated with discernment: "Brainerd's deep sense of personal unworthiness, entire dependence on Divine Grace, caused him to strive after personal holiness and holy service with an intensity that seems superhuman."

* * *

Thus Brainerd's hours in prayer were a *result* only; just as were his striving after holiness and devotion to holy service. The cause was "the mysterious constraint of Love Divine": "For the love of Christ constraineth us," that we should not henceforth live unto ourselves, but unto Him which died for us and rose again.

Saddle Bag

Album

How greatly have artists, with their pencils, brushes, engravings, and photographs, enriched the American people! The research for this volume disclosed scores of illustrations appropriate to a life of David Brainerd. About forty of the most significant have been selected for inclusion. These are grouped for you in packets, so that you may read while you ride.

Poignantly aware that the night was falling, he increased his labors in the gospel. Three powerful considerations moved upon him—the great awakening at Crossweeksung, his own physical condition, and "the mysterious constraint of Love Divine." As to the first, the Crossweeksung revival might be the omen of the Day of Visitation among the Indian tribes; and, if that were the case, the King's business required haste. As to the second, he was convinced his own life was nearing the end; whatever he could do he must do quickly. And, as to the third, his sense of gratitude to God for showing His reconciled face to one so sinful as himself, persuaded him that he was not his own; he was bought with a price! He *must* work for the night was falling!

The night was falling, indeed! Therefore, he was constantly in the saddle, agonizing his way from one wigwam village to another. The infesting afreets, anguish of body and anxiety of mind, rode constantly with him. Now and then he lifted his pale face and murmured, "O God! there is no rest but in Thee!"

Even the Narragansett pony was moved upon by the travail in the man's soul. She turned her head toward her rider and nickered softly. Of this mysterious tribute from brute creation, no one but a hard-pressed horseman may know.

(From Chapter XX, "Indian Summer")

DAVID BRAINERD
"Flagellant on Horseback"

This remarkable drawing was the work of an unknown Scottish artist sometime in the first half of the nineteenth century. Unquestionably he obtained his information concerning David Brainerd from sketches furnished by the colonial correspondents of the Society in Scotland for the Propagation of Christian Knowledge. Those early illustrators were eye witnesses, as one can readily discern in such details as the cant poles of the tepees and the slash holster of the Indian hunter.

And their drawings were trustworthy concerning Brainerd's personal appearance—the firm jaw, forward thrust, modified by the kindly eye and the uptilted face of a dreamer. One feels instinctively, "This is verily Brainerd himself! There he rides on his Narragansett, his Hebrew Lexicon on the pommel! There he rides to his tryst with duty—and death."

Almost a century ago, Partridge and Company, Ltd., of Old Bailey, London, England, published a book in which the drawing reappeared. It was our good fortune to secure a copy of this book, long since out of print. Its illustration, retouched, has been reproduced to furnish the Equestrian Portrait for this volume.

DAVID BRAINERD

1718-1747

BELL MARE

Must books always have a "preface" for heading up the chapterial cortege? Since this is a volume dealing with a horseback age, why not start it moving with a Bell Mare?

We like the equestrian sketch of David Brainerd. There he rides, always but a little ahead of death! The savage gazing after him with respectful eyes is an artistic touch suggesting the appreciation of all men, then and now, for flagellant devotion.

(Sketch Book)

ALWAYS HAS IT SEEMED ESSENTIAL, in the writing of biography, that the three of us—Deborah, Queen Elizabeth, and I—get our shadows on the lands of our subjects. Thus we followed *Man of Like Passions* from the Above All Mountain to the Forests of Lorraine; *Bush Aglow* from Northfield to Chicago's Clark Street; and a certain Bishop from Rye to Savannah. At that time a memo went into the Sketch Book:

"It is not prudent to write much about the thousands of miles we have driven in these quests, save to suggest that such journeys have woven a goodly part of life's weft. Deborah's map, marked in red, makes America appear to lie beneath a crimson gauze. We can visualize it all from the Everglades Crossing to the Boston Post Road; from Maine's little Frenchville on Number 1 to the Carolina swamps. The memories of such wayfaring constitute the treasury of things upon which men live after St. Martin's Summer has despoiled them."

* * *

Then one day thy servant said, "So many, like our missionary friends in Gadtiahi, speak well of David Brainerd; come along now and let's go find him."

We traversed wide areas in the search—from the tip of Long Island to New London; through towns and villages scattered over Connecticut. We drove across the hill country between Albany and Stockbridge, where the Taconics stand up to be admired. We dreamed through good cities like Boston, Philadelphia, and New York. We sought diligently throughout New Jersey's coastal plains where tidewater colonists settled in days of long ago.

13

"The days of long ago"! If we could find a postern gate into
yesterday, we might find him. Was not a certain doorway beneath the sycamores the surest place to restore her whose presence
long since faded away? . . . Perhaps certain men of yesterday,
who loved the land before a great nation hatched its vales and
hills with a tangle of highways, might be helpful—such as James
Fenimore Cooper.

*   *   *

"We're looking for David Brainerd, Mr. Cooper. If you could
tell us something about the ancient scenes—"

"That I can! My father brought me into the wilderness when
I was a year-old boy. I lived in a log cabin with Indians as my
familiar friends . . .

"Broad belts of the virgin wilderness, not only reached the shores of
the rivers, but even crossed them, stretching away into New England,
and affording forest covers to the noiseless moccasin of the native warrior,
as he trod the secret and bloody warpath. A bird's eye view of the whole
region east of the Mississippi must have offered one vast expanse of
woods, relieved by a comparatively narrow fringe of cultivation along
the Atlantic Ocean, dotted by the glittering surfaces of lakes, and intersected by the waving lines of rivers. In such a vast picture of solemn
solitude, the district of country we design to paint sinks into insignificance,
though we feel encouraged to proceed by the conviction that, with slight
and immaterial distinction, he who succeeds in giving an accurate idea
of any portion of this wild region must necessarily convey a tolerably
correct notion of the whole."   (The Deerslayer)

*   *   *

"The shores of the rivers"! That phrase sounded promising,
so we took to the rivers. The Connecticut, stream of Brainerd's
boyhood . . . the Delaware, scene of his early labors. We followed the Delaware through its four hundred and ten miles from
the Bay to the Catskills. We dreamed of long ago when Indians

took fine, fat shad out of its waters, with grapevine nets. . . .
But alas, though we journeyed thousands of miles, we found
him not.

*   *   *

You see, during the search, I was often repelled by certain
reports of Brainerd—his ghastly self-effacement, his habitual
melancholy, and the continuous intimations he made of dark
passages in his life. . . . Perhaps increasing prejudice blinded
my eyes; he seemed more remote as the days passed than at the
beginning.

*   *   *

And just as it began to appear that the quest was barren, we
found *ourselves* traveling the River of Frustration. At the outset
everything had been fair, brooks reflected the sun, lakes shone
back the starry skies. But of a sudden clouds and darkness moved
in. . . . We came to a place called Sunbury.

The coal towers of 1948 melted away, the ancient Indian
village called Opelhaupung returned, and Brainerd suddenly
moved into view.

He rode down a bluff, and into a glade of oaks and butternuts.
As he skirted the sassafras brush and came into a clearing, my
heart waxed heavy. I saw the lad was—dying! No longer the
carefree boy I had dreamed! The furious devotion which earlier
had lighted his face, now seamed it with furrows of care. He
coughed incessantly, his body was distressingly thin, his cheeks
sunken.

The prejudices that formerly burned towards him instantly
melted away—his habitual melancholy, terrible self-effacement,
and self-condemnation seemed no longer of weight. I was aware
only that through his labors in the forests, the oil of joy had

replaced mourning, and the garments of praise, the spirit of heaviness.

* * *

"What were your methods?" I asked respectfully, as I stood below him, close to his intelligent steed.

"I have known but one method," he said. "Travail!"

The Pennsylvania forests quickly filled with the blood-curdling yells of Red Savages, which as mysteriously changed to the Anthems of Heaven.

* * *

"Just—travail?" I stammered.

"Just—travail! There is an ancient parchment which should have long since informed you. Joel's Book of Methods has never been improved, and will never be superseded. Read it for yourself! Read where he saith: 'Turn ye even to Me, saith the Lord, with all your heart; with fasting! with weeping! with mourning! Rend your heart and not your garments! Let the ministers weep between the porch and the altar. Let them say, O Lord, spare Thy people!' "

* * *

"But," I cried (a sudden fear gripping my heart), "that sounds like Flagellantism!"

"It is!" he replied.

* * *

A sudden rushing, mighty wind sounded through the ancient forests, and I much did weep.

* * *

After a time, I heard him speak gently to his horse, "Ride on!" But in passing, he said: "Yes, it is Flagellantism. Thereon hangs the one expectancy. Why not try it? Everything else has failed. Try it! And someday the Spirit will again be poured out on all flesh. The Lord of Hosts will show wonders, even *before* the great and terrible day of the Lord! And it shall come to pass, that whosoever shall call upon the Name shall be delivered!"

*   *   *

The treasures found in the Hall of Dreams are both precious— and fearful. It is wonderful to think of the Holy One coming from Teman, His glory covering the heavens, the earth filled with His praise. But alas, have we also remembered how first the prophet had to stand upon the watch and sit upon the tower waiting to find how he should answer when he was reproved?

Likewise, it is heart-filling to remember the glory which came to the wilderness. But this volume will have eyes chiefly for the travail of the prophet which underwrote the glory.

So we returned to Cedar-Palms, having obtained an understanding of things from the very first, to write them in order. We want you to see Brainerd incessantly riding from towns to timber, and from timber to towns, indifferent alike to sultry August or frigid January. We want you to see him driven by iron devotion, retching and coughing as the plague drags him down, terribly indifferent to his own interests, careful only how he shall answer the King.

Yes, that is the order. Travail, it seems, is evermore the dark harbinger of triumph.

RICHARD E. DAY

Cedar-Palms
Sunnyvale, California
June 1, 1949

B

I

The Vanguard of Glory

(MAY 13, 1607—APRIL 20, 1718)

*When you dream about those men of yesterday,
crossing the Atlantic in a shuttle of slow-moving
wind-jammers, you cannot help thinking, "This was
the vanguard of glory!" The force of their ideals con-
quered the wilderness, and built a nation patterned
after the City of God.*

(Sketch Book)

"Thus we went out at His bidding unto a land we knew not whither. But we did know Him, and were therefore confident the future was good."

BUSKIN AND BACKDROP ARE deemed unnecessary by certain modern theaters. But we prefer good canvas behind our scenes. Likewise an account of Brainerd's countrymen, though brief, provides a proscenium for a better understanding of Brainerd himself. Our flies, floats, and footlights will consist of a handful of broad-brush sketches of Bronze Pioneers as they explored the wilderness, felled the forests, and established the institutions for a free nation. Take time, therefore, for a few portmanteau tableaux!

* * *

1607, May 13

First permanent English settlement, at Jamestown, Virginia. Jamestown was not permanent, however. Too swampy. Nothing of note remains today; there is, however, a heart-moving monument: a Cavalier looking seaward, atop a large pedestal at the mouth of the James River. This temporary settlement, nevertheless, marked an early dateline in the Birth of the Nation, and the erection of private residences too splendid for subsequent duplication. . . . Today, we put the premium upon Ranch Houses.

1609, August 28

Henry Hudson, sailing around in moonlit bays with a list of paid sightseers, warped into the mouth of the Delaware River, badly off course. His ship, the *Halve Maen,* rests at anchor while he spends "seven hours examining the banks, scenting the perfumed wilderness, and noting the big white owls." (Birds, not cheroots!) "One of the pleasantest rivers in the world," he wrote in the log. Well, that started things moving!

1609

Sir Samuel Argall, also badly off course, came to the mouth of the Delaware. He really should have been sailing Cuba-ward to get hog-meat

21

for Governor Thomas West's starving colonists in Virginia. But the Atlantic was so delightfully blue, he just sailed north instead of south. When he saw the white sand cape along the north side of Delaware Bay he named it "Cape De la Warr" (Governor West's dress-suit title). The name did not stick to the cape, but it did to the river.

1613

Three Dutch horsemen exploring the Hudson River came to the future site of Albany. They rode along the Mohawk River, and up Schoharie Creek, over the Catskill Mountains, to the headwaters of the Delaware River. Thence, down stream to the Delaware Water Gap, where a band of Minquas Indians captured them and took them to an Indian campsite. That site was exactly where Wilmington, Delaware, would one day rise.

1614

Cornelius Jacobsen Mey, of Hoorn, Holland, out on a cruise with the good ship Fortune, came to the mouth of the Delaware, and named the north sand spit "Cape Mey." That stuck, but today it is spelled "May."

1615

Mey returned to Holland, and Cornelius Henderson continued Mey's explorations, using a little sixteen tonner, the Onrush. He proceeded up the Delaware to the site of the future Philadelphia, swapped early Woolworth trinkets with the Indians for sable, otter, mink, and bear pelts. He judged the climate to be as good as Holland's, which makes us certain the month was not August. . . . They proceeded north to Christina Creek, then a beautiful stream, now a smelly thing. There they found the three captive Dutchmen, ransomed them, and set them free. Pooling their geographic knowledge, they were able to make one of those early American maps—ship off shore—for which one pays far more today than for a good Rand McNally.

1620, December 21

The Mayflower came to Plymouth Rock! And this was the real beginning of an era of commonwealth giants.

1631

Gilles Hossett, of Holland, settled near "Zwaanendael," near the present Lewes, Delaware. The name meant "Place of the Swans." These swans were actually king-sized honkers. For a time the settlers lived well on provisions gotten from the Indians—fresh Delaware sturgeon, six-inch oysters, quails, wild pigeons, deer, and turkeys. The Indians after a time killed the settlers to the last man.

1632

Pieterssen De Vries, Hossett's commanding officer, destroyed the Indian gangsters; Zwaanendael disappeared, "but it lived long enough to cause Delaware to become a separate state."

1632

First settlement at Windsor, Connecticut (Jonathan Edwards' town).

1637

Peter Minuit's motleys—ax-swinging Finns and soil-breaking Swedes —settled on the future site of Wilmington, Delaware. Here they built the first log cabin, which was destined to become just as American as ham and eggs.

1647

Saybrook and Haddam, Connecticut, settled.

1648

William Penn founded Burlington, Pennsylvania. Settlers wrote home: "Come on over! Eggs three cents a dozen. Plenty of pork, beef, fish, fowl, oysters, and cyder! Woods full of walnuts, peaches, strawberries!"

1682

Philadelphia founded. Floods of letters to Europe: "Come on over!"

1700

The Atlantic suddenly became dotted with the sails of windjammers carrying tens of thousands of settlers. By the year 1700, over *one million* have moved into the tidewater lands of the new world, their tiny settlements backed up by virgin wilderness.

1701, September

"Collegiate School of Connecticut" (Yale) founded at Saybrook. One of the co-founders was Rev. James Pierrepont, a New Haven pastor.

1703, October 5

Jonathan Edwards was born in Windsor, Connecticut.

1705

Reverend and Mrs. James Pierrepont have a daughter Sarah. She is to become Edwards' wife and Jerusha's mother. It is appropriate that Sarah Pierrepont and Jonathan Edwards are thus entered adjacent in this chronicle.

1716

Collegiate School moves to New Haven, Connecticut.

1718, April 20

David Brainerd born, Haddam, Connecticut.

1727, July 28

Jonathan Edwards married Sarah Pierrepont.

1730, April 26

Jonathan and Sarah Pierrepont Edwards have the second addition to their family, a daughter Jerusha. And it is appropriate that David Brainerd and Jerusha Edwards are recorded adjacent, just as David was later to hope he and Jerusha would be together for eternity.

1743, March 24

David Brainerd began his horseback odyssey in the wilderness.

*   *   *

By the year 1743 there are nearly two million people in the new world, their settlements scattered up and down the Atlantic seaboard. The more intrepid ones have moved from tidewater, and have built tiny, unpainted settlements in the savage wilderness. You've wasted no time, Flock of the Pages, in reading the foregoing. In fact, you should read it again. By reason of the pages just passed, you can better understand everything that follows. In the foreground there rides into the wilderness a missionary to the Indians; in the background, the lusty young civilization he has left.

II

White Spires and Colonial Homes

(AS OF AN APRIL DAY, 1718)

One would of necessity be somewhat dull if he did not think while driving through these Colonial villages: "There is something in the very architecture of these people which declares them."　　　　　(*Sketch Book*)

No part of the Brainerd research furnished memories more cherished than the visit to Haddam, Connecticut, November 3, 1948. Cold autumn rains fell intermittently as we drove from New Haven through Wallingford and Middletown. . . . Out of Middletown on Highway 9, the tumbled mountain-hills along the Connecticut River appeared. After ten miles, the ancient village of Haddam, seated on an excellent shelf of land beside the river. The two and a half centuries since Brainerd's birth only *altered* the place without *changing* it.

"So this is where Brainerd was born," mused Deborah.

The Colonial forests are gone, but the "Solitary Place" must have been just beyond Haddam, near the East Haddam bridge. Haddam must appear just about as Brainerd saw it. There are the same lovely pastoral scenes, such as "Nestledown." There are houses incredibly ancient, like "The Three Gates," built 1700. And there is a heart-moving Colonial church on Main Street. The church of Brainerd's boyhood? Perhaps not. But according to tradition, it is built on the same spot and of the same lumber.

We crossed the river on the quaint bridge. East Haddam! Here, too, Brainerd often came. Could it be that he saw that hotel? It looks old enough. . . . The whole land, mustily ancient in the fall rains, seemed precious because of Brainerd.

(Sketch Book)

CERTAINLY IT BRINGS SOME SENSE of satisfaction to find that Brainerd's ancestors did *not* arrive in America aboard the Mayflower. What do you expect? Only fifty-six males came on that trip— "forty-one gentlemen and fifteen gentleman's male servants." No doubt they were a prolific fifty-six, judging by the great number who today profess to be "Mayflower Descendants." The most optimistic view of the fertility of the Mayflower men, however, cannot account for the nearly two million settlers who lived in the New World within a hundred years after Plymouth Rock. One fact seems almost forgotten, namely, that shortly after 1620, when Europeans really began moving in on the New World, the gray sails of passenger boats were almost as numerous on the Atlantic as Hoboken ferries on the Hudson River today.

* * *

And on some of these other boats came the Hobarts and the Whitings—David's people. Rev. Peter Hobart, a Puritan refugee from Hingham, England, was David's maternal great-grandfather, as was also Rev. Samuel Whiting, who was an early settler of Boot Town, otherwise Lynn, Massachusetts. Whiting served the church at Lynn forty-one years. His wife was related to Oliver Cromwell. This links Brainerd with Puritan ancestry, and has thus provided scribblers with shining explanations — "Thus we understand David's unnaturally solemn mold—the unlovely discipline of a Calvinist child's training." Having looked, however, into the genealogies of a host of folks, we now have but casual interest in

27

the respective religious views of the ancestors. Flagellants are
found not only in the tents of Calvin, but also in the lodge of
tricksy Mr. Puck.

                               *   *   *

Suppose we start the looms as of the year 1718, and begin
at Haddam, Connecticut. If you wish to visit the village in 1950,
turn west from Highway Number 1 at Saybrook, Connecticut.
Drive fourteen miles up the Connecticut River, then look for the
white Colonial steeple. Or go, as we did, by way of Middletown.

In the year 1718, civilization is already comparatively old in
eastern Connecticut. The New England farmhouses are scattered, to be sure, but affairs are "established, not pioneer." Saybrook and Haddam have been settled for over sixty years—and
that's long enough for the appearance of youth problems in the
third generation.

Haddam was settled by folks who "liked it better inland." Over
in New Haven, another charming Colonial village, twenty-five
miles southeast on the Coast, the name "Yale" has just replaced
the name "the Collegiate School of Connecticut." The School
was founded in Saybrook, 1701, then moved to New Haven,
1716.

It is important to mention New England schools, for go where
you will in this year 1718, everyone is thinking in terms of
higher education. The ministers of the remotest villages are
college trained men. The "white spire pastor" in Haddam, a
trained man himself, is an unpaid advocate for college education.
You would be very much in error if you fancied a raw frontier
condition in this year 1718. Already bits of colored glassware
gleam alluring purples, greens and reds from their shelves in
sunny windows. Good pieces of cabinetwork, some in excellent
cherry, are to be found. Better still, these folks of Haddam in

the year 1718, as in the whole area of the thirteen states, have amazing ideas of democracy, and cherish as a symbol of their best hopes "their sweet spires pointing upward in the woodland."

Now let us walk eastward from Haddam a short distance to a certain farm lying on the bluff above the Connecticut River; a few acres of soil just right for gardening, fringed about with clumps of heavy woodland. Remember this woodland! Right there is located a certain "Solitary Place" of which we shall soon have more to say. The good man and wife on this farm are Hezekiah and Dorothy Brainerd. Hezekiah was evidently a farmer of parts: was he not one of His Majesty's Council for the Colony, a sort of country squire?

His wife, Dorothy, also is well connected. Was not her father the sturdy old preacher, Rev. Jeremiah Hobart? Sereno Edwards Dwight, whose *Memoirs of the Rev. David Brainerd* light many dark places for our account, tells us about the life of Rev. Jeremiah Hobart. He preached awhile at Topsfield, then took a work at Hempstead, Long Island. But "so many villagers turned Quakers and so many others being so irreligious" [sic!], that Preacher Hobart had the option of seeing his family starve or of accepting the call to the Haddam Church. He selected Haddam, "where he died in the eighty-fifth year of his age. He went to Church in the forenoon, and died in his chair between meetings."

Dwight also opens the old records so that we may witness a church romance. Daniel Brainerd, a village justice of the peace, also a deacon in the Haddam Church—the Church of Christ— had a son, Hezekiah. And Hezekiah Brainerd had a mind to Preacher Hobart's daughter, Dorothy, which brings us right back to Hezekiah and Dorothy Brainerd!

But before the moving pen moves on, it is quite in order to write about the incredible flock of preachers there were on David's

mother's side of the house. Not only was her father, Jeremiah
Hobart, a preacher, but her grandfather also, Peter Hobart, was
a preacher. Rev. Peter Hobart began his ministry at Hingham,
England. When persecutions of the Puritans began, he fled with
his family and settled in Hingham, Massachusetts.

And Peter Hobart had five sons, *four* of whom were preachers!
—Jeremiah (Dorothy's father), above named; Joshua; Gershom;
and Nehemiah. Did these three preachers, Dorothy's uncles, have
preacher sons? Deponent sayeth not. But we do know a little
about Dorothy's mother. She was a daughter of Rev. Samuel
Whiting, first a minister in Boston, England; later a pastor in
Lynn, Massachusetts. And into the parsonage of Samuel Whiting,
at Lynn, came three sons, Dorothy Brainerd's uncles, who were
preachers! Dorothy, in turn, maintained the ministerial score in
giving to the Colonies nine children, five boys and four girls.
And four of her five sons became ministers—Nehemiah, David,
John, and Israel! Nehemiah Brainerd was a minister at Eastbury,
Connecticut, and "died of a consumption Nov. 10, 1742," at the
age of twenty-seven. Of David, John, and Israel this account has
more to say. John (February 20, 1720—March 18, 1781) "died
of a good old age." Israel (1722—March 6, 1748) died while a
student at Yale. . . . Hezekiah Brainerd, Jr. (David's brother)
side-stepped the ministry and became, like his father, a country
squire; later, a representative in the general assembly of Massachusetts.

But the above discloses that David Brainerd could look into
the old album in the sitting room—if they had one!—and see
the pictures of at least fourteen near-in male relatives who were
preachers!

No one apparently felt it was necessary to tell us about
David's aunts—Dorothy's sisters—if perchance they married and

mothered preachers; or if David's four sisters married and mothered preachers. We know of Miss Spencer Brainerd only, David's favorite sister. She married a Haddam farm boy, and died in her early thirties "of a consumption," June, 1747. And Spencer was as a mother in Israel!

* * *

Some, taking into account David's many preacher relatives, have tried thus to explain his unnaturally solemn frame of mind. There's no connection. Others have tried to explain Brainerd's melancholy by pointing to his Puritan forebears. That, too, is a non-sequitur! . . . And still others explain David's almost continuous depression on the ground that he was afflicted "with a consumption." Still illogical. There was the Cactus Curate, Billy Percival, for instance, whose annals are yet to appear in *Jack Highheels*. Billy, despite white plague, took life by the hand and romped with it until the angels came to get him.

* * *

Having thus set our scenes, we are ready for the twentieth day of April, 1718. For on the night of that day, Dorothy Brainerd travailed again, and gave to her third son what she esteemed the sweetest boy-name she had ever heard: the name of an ancient shepherd lad of whom her father, Rev. Jeremiah Hobart, delighted to preach in the Haddam Church—"David"!

Packet 2

EARLY AMERICAN

"Broad belts of the virgin wilderness, not only reached the shores of the rivers, but even crossed them, stretching away into New England, and affording forest covers to the noiseless moccasin of the native warrior, as he trod the secret and bloody warpath. A bird's-eye view of the whole region east of the Mississippi must have offered one vast expanse of woods, relieved by a comparatively narrow fringe of cultivation along the Atlantic Ocean, dotted by the glittering surfaces of lakes, and intersected by the waving lines of rivers. In such a vast picture of solemn solitude, the district of country we design to paint sinks into insignificance, though we feel encouraged to proceed by the conviction that, with slight and immaterial distinction, he who succeeds in giving an accurate idea of any portion of this wild region must necessarily convey a tolerably correct notion of the whole.

—From *The Deerslayer*, by
JAMES FENIMORE COOPER (1789-1851)

Engraving by William H. Bartlett (1809-1854). Courtesy Wyoming Historical and Geological Society.

VIEW OF THE SUSQUEHANNA

"One vast expanse of woods, intersected by the waving lines of rivers."

●

STATUE, JAMES FENIMORE COOPER
Cooperstown, New York

"We're looking for Mr. Brainerd, Mr. Cooper. If you could tell us something of the ancient scenes. . . ."

"That I can! My father brought me into this wilderness when I was a year-old boy."
(Bell Mare)

●

FOREST SCENE ON THE TOBIHANNA

"The Tobihanna—the upper waters of the Lehigh River, formerly called the West Branch of the Delaware."

"Broad belts of virgin wilderness, stretching away into New England."

Aquatint by Karl Bodmer (1809-1893), a Swiss artist; drawn on his travels in North America with Maximilian, Prince of Wied. Courtesy, Wyoming Historical and Geological Society, Wilkes-Barre, Pennsylvania.

III

Yankee Farm Boy

(1718-1738)

These New England children, who developed in time the Bah Habah drawl, had in their minds and hearts certain traits passed on from their ancestors. There was, for instance, one settler, Perceval Lowle, who came to Newberry, Massachusetts, in 1639. In Perceval there was a capacity for clowning and a capacity for lofty flight. These he passed down the complicated branches of the Lowell tree, cotyledonlike, until they reappeared two centuries later in a Lowell named Amy and another named James Russell. And both got into trouble by mixing clowning and soaring. . . . But certainly the mordant for all the traits that summed up "Yankee" was the Puritan faith.

(Sketch Book)

c

THE Yankee temperament came out of the pioneer melting pot; and since it did, no man may say it's British, or Dutch, or Swedish, or what! It's just— Yankee! (Sketch Book)

DETAIL CONCERNING THE BOYHOOD of David Brainerd is exceedingly meager, and regrettably deficient in those accounts which tell how the world impressed a young lad.

There is nothing corresponding to Spurgeon's boyhood memories, such as the fragrance of a freshly clipped yew hedge in a spring shower. Nothing about shad fishing along the Connecticut River; or how delicious the bony, white flesh tasted to a growing child. There is no record concerning the spicy life of Mr. Woody Woodpecker as he fussed around in the treetops. There was no place in Brainerd's thinking for the pungent husks of Fall butternuts; or the flight of purple martins, which mysteriously appeared in late May and as mysteriously disappeared in early August.

In fact, Brainerd's lack of interest in the objective world continued until he was through with it. You read along in his later records, hoping he will tell you about the way two Creek Indians built their captivating wigwams, but he never does. From the outset he moved in a world where moods were of greater interest than mountains, and frames had much more value than Connecticut forests flaming with October gold. As to Brainerd's early years, we must remain content with but little more than a line or so: "He was a melancholy boy with a religious disposition."

* * *

Three old books lie on the desk before me, all retrieved from the tailings of a secondhand bookstore in Gotham. These are

35

the standard volumes upon the life of David Brainerd: Jonathan
Edwards' *Account;* Sereno Edwards Dwight's "complete" *Memoirs;*
and James M. Sherwood's *Memoirs of Brainerd.* There is also
The Life and Diary of David Brainerd, printed by the Moody
Press, 1949. This latter is to our day what Sherwood's book was
to his.*

None of these books contains satisfactory information upon
Brainerd's childhood and teen age. What little there is comes
from the *Memoirs:*

> His father died in 1726, when he was but a child of eight. This pro-
> duced a crisis of faith. He became concerned, terrified at the thought of
> death; was driven to the performance of religious duties; but that was
> a melancholy business destroying his eagerness for play . . . the concern
> was short-lived.

The second experience came after he was thirteen, in February,
1732:

> He had been reading Janeway's *Token for Children.* This and a mortal
> sickness in Haddam roused him out of his carnal security and he became
> melted in the duties of religion. As a climactic factor his mother died
> in March, 1732, and the "numerous" family was scattered. All of this
> brought him to a point where he might indeed say, "Almost I was per-
> suaded to be a Christian." But—he fell back!

*   *   *

After his mother's death, he "lived on a farm near East Haddam"—probably with the Spencers.

"East Haddam?" said Deborah. "Why, that's just across the
Connecticut River."

So we drove over the quaint bridge. Right on the riverbank
stood an old hotel, so shabby we could easily have believed

Brainerd saw it; yet, apparently, Mr. Duncan Hines never did!

The hills press close to the river, so that the road running north begins a steep ascent as soon as you leave the hotel and its satellite stores. Six miles back of East Haddam there is a small tract called "Brainard Homestead State Park." * But it does not appear that this farm can be connected with David Brainerd. This particular Brainard was a modern. He lived only a hundred years ago. A dentist by profession, he gave the early citizens some excellent bridgework.

"Was he related to Brainerd?" The baffling antiquity of Haddam Land quickly discourages interviews. "David Brainerd?" they say. "Never heard of him." One of the habitants did brighten up—"Say, wasn't he a sort of Indian missionary?" The country seems as unrelated to the present, or the past, as the eddies in the Wabash River at the Second Sand Bar. Suddenly you recall, "After all, Brainerd's birth was nearly two hundred and fifty years ago!"

There on the East Haddam farm Brainerd "lived for about four years"—that volcanic zone from fourteen to eighteen. But David himself seems never to have become volcanic:

> He was not much addicted to frolicking company, and even when he sometimes went, his good frames were spoiled, so he did not go often.

Two words in the preceding deserve special attention. "Frames," in those days, was as serviceable a term as "mood" today. Jonathan Edwards used the word so frequently he nearly wore the milling from it. . . . Of the phrase "frolicking company" no clear idea has yet emerged. Sometimes, in Edwards' pages, it seems to be almost equivalent to "petting party," or a Texas barn

---

* This spelling, "Brainard" instead of "Brainerd," was projected by an early misspelling of David's surname. Many little American communities, seeking to honor Brainerd, got off to a bad start by following the incorrect spelling!

dance. It may be quite a surprise to some, though it shouldn't be, to learn that Puritans knew anything about such matters!

*   *   *

In April, 1737, near his nineteenth birthday, David "went to work on his own farm at Dedham," which was about ten miles from Haddam, and twenty miles from Yale. As to how this farm was acquired, its size, no data is available. In fact the latest Rand McNally road map does not even show Dedham. We would be satisfied if you said it was near Durham Center, east of Wallingford. There, as he plowed and planted, "dreams of a liberal education began to fill his mind." He is careful to affirm, however, that these dreams were "from mere natural principles," and that while on his farm (still unconverted) "he decided to enter the ministry." "He became strict and watchful over his thoughts and actions, applied himself more assiduously to the duties of religion, and concluded he was *sober* [sic!] because he designed to become a minister." This accounts for his leaving the farm, after less than a year, and returning to Haddam.

*   *   *

The pastor of the church on Haddam's Main Street, Rev. Thaddeus Fiske, was a fiery advocate of a liberal education, and an old friend of the Brainerds. Likely he succeeded David's grandfather, Jeremiah Hobart, as the church's pastor. He called at the Brainerd Farm to welcome David home. "If David wished, Mr. Fiske could start him on a course of study, and David could live at the manse." During the balance of the year 1737, therefore, David lived with Mr. Fiske.

He again became deeply interested in matters of religion, and read the Bible through twice in the year. On Sabbath nights, he "companied with other serious boys for religious exercises." When he later went to his room, "he meditated upon the day's sermons, and reviewed them again Monday mornings."

In November, 1737, when Mr. Fiske died, David moved again to the Brainerd Farm, where Sister Spencer and Brother John were living. John, too, like his older brothers, Nehemiah and David, entertained ministerial aspirations, so David and John continued their studies in company, farming as they went.

Brainerd records that he maintained "a strict round of duties— Bible reading, self-examination and prayer." But despite all these appearances, he was unsaved. By reason of his "good outside, he actually went a considerable length on a self-righteous foundation, entirely lost and undone had not the mercy of God prevented."

* * *

Should anyone judge that the trip to Haddam Land produced but little material, we would reply, "Though it were ten times as difficult, we would do it again!" The Connecticut River flowing between its hills-strewn banks, the ancient land, the very scenes Brainerd looked upon, made him seem real indeed. In fact, one little sentence was sufficient reward for the whole journey:

Being slender, he appeared tall, and was withal attractive in appearance. His dark brooding eyes and quiet demeanor instantly drew one's attention.

IV

A Solitary Place

(1738-1739)

Wherein a record, purloined from an ancient volume, is set forth, which will, we hope, by means of fastening modern eyes upon yesterday, greatly help in resolving a certain critical problem of today.

"One morning I was walking in a solitary place. . . ."
"I walked out again into the same place. . . ."

(Memoirs)

The new birth of David Brainerd is one of the best case records in the Romance of the Twice Born, the sublunary scene of which was a certain Solitary Place.

There was a patch of Middlesex woodland shouldering against the cleared acres of the Brainerd farm near Haddam, Connecticut. One portion, just beyond the copse, stood from ancient days untouched by edged tools. Here it was that the lad experienced the mystery of Heaven, whereof the cold April winds, blowing as they listed through the budding tops of hard maples, became a symbol. No man knew whence those spring zephyrs came or whither they went. But what matter? Here, he was born from above. (Sketch Book)

EVANGELS IN BROAD BRIMS, among whom the Brainerds lived, used a term for the new birth which could scarcely be misunderstood. They designated that final and transforming experience through which a man was "born from above" as "the effective call." Therein they set forth in a phrase the eternal difference between the superficial emotional experiences of unregenerate men and that crowning event which never needed to be—in fact, never could be—repeated:

> " 'Tis done! the great transaction's done!
> I am my Lord's, and He is mine."

*   *   *

David passed through several of these "inconclusive religious intervals" between the ages of eight and twenty; but so far as he was concerned, he remained "without God and without hope in the world." * The "effective call" (excellent bit of verbal Paisley!) came to Brainerd about the time of his twenty-first birthday.

Discerning men universally agree that Brainerd's *Memoirs* are the most interesting works of the kind ever written; and that a host of persons, such as Robert Murray M'Cheyne and Henry Martyn, were "integrated" by the reading of them. A little closer attention makes it clear that one of the chief factors which gave

---

* A number of writers have felt Brainerd was "unfair with himself; he was converted early in life, and that which took place at twenty-one was 'a deeper experience.' " Such writers not only prove themselves inept soul-surgeons, but also set themselves against the judgment of Jonathan Edwards and of Brainerd himself.

such power to the *Memoirs* is Brainerd's infinite care to distinguish between mere "good frames" and his final "new heart," without which no man has either joy, effectiveness, or perseverance in the King's vineyard. This record—how he fared through mere emotions to real knowledge—will be a valued Christian document to the end of time. Of this we now think.

* * *

On a certain Sabbath morning in December, 1738, as he walked in "the Solitary Place, it pleased God on a sudden to give him such a sense of his danger, and the wrath of God, that he stood amazed, and his former good frames were reduced to nothing." This revealed to him his sin and vileness, and brought him to great distress, in which he lived constantly from day to day. He continued to "perform his duties" with a secret hope that these might recommend him to God. At times, when he had great meltings of heart, he imagined God must be as much melted as he, and surely would heed his sincere cries. Thus, throughout December of 1738, and January of 1739, he agonized, trying "to heal his distresses with his duties."

In early February, 1739, he set apart a whole day for secret fasting, that "he might find the way of life in Jesus Christ." The "Solitary Place" was locked in winter's chains. A few coppered leaves blew over the deep snow. It was a day of terrible struggle—"O God, what *qualifications* must I have to be saved?" (not, "What must I do?")

The balance of February and March dragged by. Winter's hold began to slacken. Crows appeared in the leafless branches of the naked trees. . . . One night in March, he had such a view of his sin, "he feared the ground would cleave under his feet and become his grave; he hurried to bed, lest brother John see his agitation." It came to him that restless night when he felt so distressed, that agitation itself would commend him to God. This brought fresh hope—"God will regard my distress"—filled him with a sense of carnal security, and "his conviction of sin grew languid. This alarmed him anew." As a result, he fell into a horrible frame of contesting with the Almighty, and his way of dealing with mankind. Particularly, he revolted against the imputation of Adam's sin to his posterity, and most particularly, *to himself!*

*   *   *

The next phase of this struggle revolved about the doctrine of the sovereignty of God. That doctrine of men of his day was not primarily conceived as the glorious thesis, "God has a right to rule." When the doctrine of sovereignty was mentioned to an eighteenth-century man, he immediately thought of a singularly limited and academic corollary: "God has a right to approve or damn any man, all men, and does! even before they are born! No man can be saved unless he is reconciled to being damned!" The very thought of this he couldn't bear; he went to war against such texts as Romans 9:11:

"For the children being not yet born, neither having done any good or evil, that the purpose of God according to election might stand, NOT OF WORKS, BUT OF HIM THAT CALLETH."

Only expository ingenuity could Charley McCarthy that text into saying that God *actually does elect* some to damnation; but in David's day it was a mental squirrel cage filled with terrible non sequiturs. Today there are other squirrel cages. We once met certain children distressed over the thesis that God, if He wished, had a right to turn men into hoptoads! When amusement ends, we perceive that such gratuitous anguish is apt to rise

within any man who strives to enter the narrow gate; any man
in the process of wild threshings to avoid the basic truth:

> "Naught have I gotten
> But what I received;
> Grace hath bestowed it
> Since I have believed;
> Boasting excluded,
> Pride I abase;
> I'm only a sinner
> Saved by grace!"
>
> (James M. Gray)

*   *   *

As a "final desperate maneuver of the flesh," Brainerd decided
to assault God on an academic front: he would attain a frame
of being willing that God should condemn him, and leave the
outcome in God's hand. But he would wait until his "frames
were so sweet" that it was reasonably certain God would not
condemn him. . . . Before he could bring this to pass, however,
a terrible alternative appeared:

Suppose, having become willing to be damned, God *did* damn him;
then he himself had approved his damnation!

*   *   *

Wild projects now thronged his mind; "projects full of atheism
to thwart God's designs, or even to escape His notice." Realizing
such schemes were impossible, he then wished there were no
God, or another God that could control Him. This he sensed at
once was blasphemy—a horrible thought. He never in the world
set out to have such rebellious notions, but "they were *his* notions,
and proved him by nature an enemy of God."

Once he had revolted against Mr. Edwards' terrible statement that unregenerate men were enemies of God, and would kill Him if they could. He esteemed his own heart not quite so bad as either Mr. Edwards or the Bible affirmed. Now he plainly saw he was as sinful as any! and—God wouldn't be safe in his hands for an hour!

On the Sunday evening of April 15, 1739, the boy walked the Solitary Place with a noose about his neck. "He was lost. All his past praying, pretending, fasting, heaped up before God were a sham and a mockery; a horrid abuse of God. All his contrivances to gain salvation had been in vain, and would be in vain though magnified a thousand times with all eternity in which to work. He was hopelessly lost." The battle was lost, and so was he. When he came to this dark conclusion, strangely enough, "the tumult quieted."

* * *

It may seem a literary throwback to set a chapter like this into a modern book. But you are advised, Flock of the Pages, get the *Memoirs,* and read detail not mentioned here. A galaxy of pilgrims have been thankful that Brainerd made such a record of his struggles—and theirs!

* * *

There remains but that last phase, that which maketh the angels to rejoice—

"God be merciful to me a sinner!"

Packet 3

HADDAM LAND

"So this is where Brainerd was born!" mused Deborah.

The Colonial forests are gone. But Haddam must appear today just about as Brainerd saw it; the same lovely pastoral scenes . . . the whole land mustily ancient in the Fall rains, seemed precious because of Brainerd.

"NESTLEDOWN," HADDAM

"There are lovely pastoral scenes which help visualize the 'Solitary Place.'"

FIRST CONGREGATIONAL CHURCH HADDAM

"There is a heart-moving Colonial church on the Main Street. The church of Brainerd's boyhood? the one of which his grandfather, Rev. Jeremiah Hobart, was pastor? where Hezekiah and Dorothy, his parents, courted and were married? Perhaps not; but according to tradition, it is 'built on the same spot and of the same lumber.'"

JOSEPH ARNOLD HOUSE, HADDAM
Built 1700

"The two and a half centuries since Brainerd's birth have only altered the place without changing it."

V

Dark Grove:
Unspeakable Glory

(APRIL 22, 1739)

*He walks into the darkest part of
the Solitary Place, and is amazed when
he comes upon a Light above the brightness of the sun.*

D

"At midday, O king, I saw in the way a light from heaven."—*Acts 26:13*.

FOR THE ENTIRE WEEK FOLLOWING
Sunday, April 15, 1739, even to his twenty-first birthday, Friday,
April 20, David walked the Solitary Place, no hope in his heart.
On Sunday evening, April 22, he walked again. The account
of "this poor man" has strange power over the heart. We know
what is about to happen to him, even though he does not, and
no drama ever had more "pick-up." David, you tell us about it.

I continued in this state of mind till Sabbath evening, when I was
walking again in the same solitary place, where I was brought to see
myself lost. . . . I was attempting to pray; but found no heart to engage
in it. My former religious affections were now gone . . . nothing in
heaven or earth could make me happy.

He thus walked "for near half an hour," the glories of a Spring
sunset in New England faded away. Insensibly he walked into
the darkest thicket of the grove. What difference? What could
be darker than his own heart? And then—speak on, David!
thine is a twice-told tale of which, though we should live another century, we would never tire:

Having thus been endeavoring to pray—very stupid and senseless, I
was walking in a dark, thick grove . . . [then] *unspeakable glory seemed
to open to my soul.* I do not mean any external brightness, for I saw
no such thing! It was a new view I had of God, such as I had never seen
before, nor anything like it.
I stood still, wondered! I had no particular apprehension of any one
Person in the Trinity, either the Father, the Son, or the Holy Ghost—it
was Divine Glory! My soul rejoiced with joy unspeakable to see such
a God. I was infinitely pleased and satisfied that He should be God over
all forever and ever!

51

There now, David, you're qualified upon the doctrine of sovereignty; but you qualified because you *were* saved; you did not qualify first, then receive salvation. Please excuse us, young friend, we are so moved listening to you. Pray, go on.

My soul was so captivated with the perfections of God that I was even swallowed up in Him. I had no thought about my own salvation, and scarce reflected there was such a creature as myself. Thus I was brought to a hearty disposition to exalt Him! . . . to set Him on the throne! . . . to aim at His honor and glory as King of the Universe. I felt myself in a new world, and everything appeared different.

Now, David, with all your Bible reading, you surely know you're practically quoting Scripture—"If any man is in Christ Jesus there is a new creation!" Excuse, please! He seems to say in the *Memoirs,* "Not so fast, my friend: I was just coming to that."

At the same time, the way of salvation opened to me with such infinite wisdom that I wondered I should ever think of any other way of salvation . . . so lovely, blessed, excellent! If I could have been saved as I formerly contrived it, my soul would now have refused it. . . . The sweet relish of what I found continued several days, almost constantly.*

That "sweet relish"—anyone who knows of it never forgets! For the next several days, when the light of Spring dawn entered the farm bedroom at Haddam, he, like Finney, arose to his knees in bed—"He was saved! through no merit of his own! just saved by grace!" After a week, this joy unspeakable changed from the similarity of a tumultuous mountain stream to the strong, steady flow of a river; just like his own Delaware when its wild power in the Catskills quieted down to the strong, steady flow at Easton.

Throughout May and June this quiet joy continued; then into

---

* Brainerd states that *Guide to Christ* was "a happy means to his conversion." This book was written by Edwards' grandfather, Solomon Stoddard.

New England summer, July and August. Oh, to be sure, as Mr. Edwards said of him, he remained "the most melancholy person I ever met"; he continued to pass through days of fathomless depression. But never again were these depressions related to the query, "Am I saved, or am I lost?" He maintained an abiding sense of personal unworthiness and unmerited grace.

His feet at last by Sovereign Grace were set on that great Rock Foundation. From now on, no mountains appointed by the will of God were too rugged for passage, no "deserts" too dark, no winters too bitter! All lashes falling upon his back, as he labored for His dear sake, were of no more consequence than the pelting of snowflakes!

* * *

Are not memorials of birth as important as memorials of death? Would that a bit of Vermont granite were set up on the Connecticut River just east of Haddam, in the Solitary Place, upon whose side this text were graven:

"Near Here,
April 22, 1739,
David Brainerd
Was
Born from Above"

VI

Yale Cropper

(SEPTEMBER, 1739—FEBRUARY, 1742)

In which we see how odious Mr. Warm Heart appeareth to Mr. Luke Warm, and how inappropriately at times, with due apologies to Messrs. Gilbert and Sullivan, the crime is fitted to the punishment.

"The archers shot at him and wounded him, but his bow abode in strength."

UIDED WITH THE PURPOSE OF furnishing himself completely unto the work of the ministry, Brainerd "entered Yale College September, 1739." He doubted his ability to lead a life of strict religion in the midst of temptations incident to student life. He knew Yale was then in a spendthrift era of morals, money, and wit; but this was not what he feared. The hours of study required were the dangerous factors: these might cause him to lose the sweet relish of faith and grow dull towards religion.*

However, through Fall and into December, it pleased God to visit his soul with clearer manifestations of Himself; he constantly enjoyed considerable sweetness. He maintained the glow by a continued use of solitude. "He loved to walk abroad and repeatedly engage in prayer." The cherished Solitary Place at Haddam was immediately replaced by a tract of woodland just north of the Yale campus—today a very populous area of New Haven. This became an all-year chapel for his devotions, whether January gloom or June glory.

There were also other helps. For instance, it was an easy ride from the campus to the Congregational Church in the meadows at Ripton, east of Derby. There, dear Mr. Mills was pastor; and Jedediah Mills, though but a few years Brainerd's senior, was an inspiration. He was a Yale graduate, a splendid scholar, and a godly pastor. To converse with him, to kneel with him in

* We trust the reader will identify many of the quaint expressions used in this book, without benefit of quotation marks, as being the language of Brainerd himself: such phrases as "strict religion," "sweet relish of faith," and the like.

prayer, always sent David back to his studies with a heart flaming like a fire-pan.

*   *   *

In January, 1740, an epidemic of measles swept the campus. Brainerd, during his youth on the farm, had always been depressed by sickness in others, so now he felt greatly deserted. But just before he was himself stricken, he had, during one of his forest walks, a sweet, refreshing visit, he trusted, from above, and he was raised beyond the fears of death.

After he contracted measles, he became so ill he was obliged to return to the Haddam farm. And there, in the ancient haunts, his affection for God flamed brighter than ever. During a Communion Service in the dear old church on Main Street, his soul was filled with light and love as he looked on the sacramental elements. He was in ecstasy, though his body was so weak he could scarcely stand . . . he longed to be freed from all sin. . . . When he thought of going back to college and its attendant dangers of getting away from God, he would rather have died. . . . However, in late January, he returned to Yale.

*   *   *

But the rowdy atmosphere among the students disturbed him more than he thought it would. It was like poison. One day in June, 1740, he walked beyond his forest to a considerable distance. There in the fields alone, he found unspeakable sweetness in God: the vulgar life of the students presumed to be Christians seemed unintelligible—and intolerable. He felt obliged to isolate himself from it. Therefore he decided to plunge into hard study.

But this was a serious mistake. He greatly wronged his health and his spirituality. Right at this juncture, as Barrie would have phrased it, the small black spot appeared which was to get him in the end. The disease which ran in his family was provoked. It was to shorten his life, and make what remained a continuous anguish. In August he began to spit blood.

* * *

In November, 1740, he returned to Yale; but alas! unmindful of his August breakdown, he resumed student labors with such added zeal that by January, 1741, the dreaded White Plague was fixed upon him. There now appear in the *Memoirs* early examples of those shocking entries which bemoan his personal wickedness—"he bitterly mourned over his great vileness." What sin was it that distressed him? You are mystified by such sentiments.

* * *

However, just at this time a helpful counteractant appeared. In February, 1741, the fires of the Great Awakening waxed very strong and general in New Haven. Certain young gentlemen of Yale, given to profligacy, were changed overnight, and became paragons of decency. The sight of men born again rescued Brainerd from his despondent apathy and lifted him to his former sweet relish. He was carried right out of a proper scholarly restraint in matters of religion, and moved over into the Hallelujah Section of the Church. Indeed, we must confess, "he became noisy."

* * *

September 15, 1741, there was an event at the graduation exercises of considerable interest to Brainerd. The very noted alumnus, Mr. Jonathan Edwards, appeared as the preacher of the baccalaureate sermon. The Great Awakening was running full tide. It was surprising that Yale invited Edwards to speak, since he was known to admire Mr. Whitfield. Indeed Whitfield had preached for Edwards five times in the Northampton Church. One who admired nonconformists to that degree was not generally invited to speak at Yale, especially under Rector Clap.

But Brainerd, junior classman, was enraptured. This was the first time he ever saw Mr. Edwards; and if anyone after due subordination to Jesus could be used as a life model, that is what Mr. Edwards was to him. He read everything he could find, written by Mr. Edwards; in fact, his religious experiences and phraseology were unconsciously copies of Edwards'.

Edwards' baccalaureate sermon was conceived as a liaison effort. He would speak upon the subject of "Revivals," justifying them on the one hand by their results; warning, on the other hand, against their emotional excesses, even if it came to reproving Mr. Whitfield. Thus, everyone would be pleased. Actually, few were.

*   *   *

The importance of the Great Awakening to this narrative deserves a distilled paragraph. That event was a six-year blaze of revival glory (1739-1745), whereby the entire course of New England history was markedly affected. It began in a series of disjoined awakenings. Jonathan Edwards had one in the Northampton Church, 1734. There was another, 1736, in New Jersey under the ministries of William and Gilbert Tennent; still another, 1738, under Jonathan Dickinson at Newark; and one in Harvard, 1739, with fiery John Seccomb preaching.* George Whitfield heaped the residual embers together, added fresh fuel, and by means

---

* One of the most cherished Cedar-Palms volumes covering this matter is *Great Revivals and the Great Republic*, Chandler, Publishing House of the M. E. Church, South, 1904.

of his golden voice, capable of being heard in an open-air meeting by twenty thousand people, produced a conflagration of glory.

* * *

All of the foregoing is introductory to the tragic disgrace which came upon Brainerd. The chief factor was the newly installed (April 2, 1740) young Rector (President) of Yale, Rev. Thomas Clap. He "nauseated revivals and detested Whitfield." Some explained this on the ground that Clap was "a rigid Calvinist." Actually he was simply "rigid." He is described as "a little bumblebee who tried to appear a forceful eagle; an irascible, high-handed, thickset bully." When he left the pastorate of the Congregational Church at Windham, Massachusetts, to become president of Yale, "the congregation acted like boys let out of school." Thus he began an irritated administration of the college: "a great executive must exhibit great severity"! He frowned and scolded, got a few new buildings constructed; but finally, 1763, "was removed on the ground that he was in his dotage."

The invasion of the Yale campus by the Great Awakening made the young president fighting mad. To be frank, he was generally fighting mad, but—"Revivals!"—they brought him such a temperature that he could no longer be a gentleman! This hallelujah business had to be stopped. The students were revival crazed, demoralized! Actually trooping out of town, going down the coast to Milford to hear Gilbert Tennent! (Others were going over to Milford on account of the excellent schnapps; but that was different.) The Rector issued a stern order against attending nonconformist meetings, and waiting for the appearance of a whipping boy.

But alas! when the whipping boy appeared, he was none other than mild David Brainerd. He did not look mild to the Rector. Rumor came that Brainerd was attending separatist meetings. Actually, Brainerd attended but once. Rumor added fuel: "Brainerd said he marvelled the Rector didn't fall dead for issuing such an order." Actually, he never dreamed of such a statement. Another thing: under the impact of the Awakening, certain students "in order to mutual assistance in spiritual things," consorted as "The New Lights." Rumor said, "Brainerd is one of them." He was.

By that time the Rector, beetle-browed, was crouched for the kill. Then one day came the occasion. Two or three New Lights tarried in the hall after chapel. One said to Brainerd, "What do you think of Mr. Whittelsey?" Whittelsey was a Yale tutor with just enough religion to make him miserable. When he had been called upon that morning to lead chapel prayer, he, conscious of the atmosphere of revival zeal, had essayed to make himself acceptable to man and to God. Edwards said his prayer was "unusually pathetic."

Brainerd answered the question with adolescent candor. He put his hand upon a chapel seat, and said, "He has no more grace than this chair."

That was no mere peccadillo, Page Flock! We offer no apology. What an awful remark to make of an inoffensive chair! . . . Some student passing in the hall overheard it. He promptly told a town's lady. She hurried to the Rector's office and reported the remark to him.

"To whom did he refer?" roared the Rector.

"No names were mentioned," responded the lady.

"Well, *I* know," fumed the Rector. "The general description is sufficient!"

Breathing threatenings and slaughter, the Rector demanded of Brainerd that he apologize before faculty and students. Brainerd, we are delighted to find, refused. Clap stormed before a special session of the Yale governors, and with their "approval" expelled Brainerd from school in the month of February, 1742.*

* * *

We are bound to consider carefully Brainerd's expulsion. His two and a half student years had already gained for him recognition as the valedictorian of the Class of 1743. But now his student days suddenly end in disgrace! His subsequent grief accounts for a signal increase of his abject melancholy, and of the pitiful self-loathing which abounds in his *Memoirs;* more particularly, it accounts for his transformation into a thoroughgoing flagellant. He carried the scars of this cropper until his death. But, there was also fused into his soul by this same misfortune those qualities whereby he crashed the brazen gates of Paganism, and implanted among the wigwams the Light of the World.

* Later, however, Brainerd after his expulsion did apologize—a needless humiliation.

Packet 4

BRAINERD'S HEBREW LEXICON

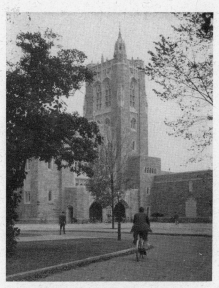

HARVEY S. FIRESTONE LIBRARY
PRINCETON UNIVERSITY
*Photo, courtesy Department
of Rare Books*

"Little did Brainerd dream, when he spent the night of September 19, 1746, in the home of Pastor Stockston, of the University which someday would rise in the woodland near the Princeton manse. And little could he dream of the magnificent library building in which his relics would be cherished treasures."

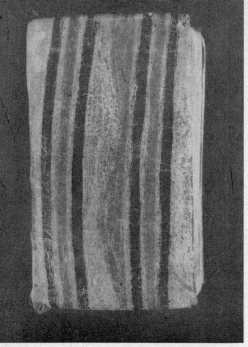

BRAINERD'S HEBREW LEXICON

Photos, Courtesy the Department of Rare Books, Harvey S. Firestone Library, Princeton University.

This Hebrew Lexicon, one of the most valued Protestant relics, is now in the Library of Princeton University, Department of Rare Books and Special Collections. When Brainerd died, the book became the property of Jonathan Edwards. When Edwards died, it was passed on to the college which later was called Princeton. Through the kindness of Howard C. Rice, Jr., head of the Rare Books Department, and of Miss Caroline Hiatt (now Mrs. Dixon), former head, the microfilm pictures were made which afford the public for the first time a photograph of the volume.

The Lexicon is three inches thick, four and one-eighth inches wide, six and three-quarters inches high. Constant "riding reference" during Brainerd's horseback Odyssey tattered the covers. The Indians at Crossweeksung "rebound" it. They used a piece of otter skin from which they had scuffed the hair with clam shells, then "decorated" it with bands of raw pigment. The color of the ochre stripes from left to right are black, red, black, red, black, red, black.

It was indeed treading on holy ground when, November 3, 1948, the University authorities turned the Lexicon over to us for examination.

THE LEXICON OPENED AT PAGES 529-528

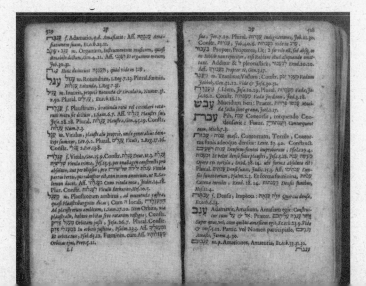

VII

A Flagellant Is Born
(APRIL 20, 1742)

It is unwise to disvalue flagellants—their names appear too frequently in the Romance of Faith; such men as Judson and Taylor, Bingham and Bernard of Clairvaux. The flagellants reappear in every age where impossible labors must be done. You can step back across Christian history from one flagellant to another until you finally come to the Source of them all. You hear Him say, "He that loseth his life for My sake shall find it"; then see Him stretch out His arms to die upon a Roman gibbet.

Suddenly contempt shrinks back abashed. Conscience whispers, "It may be the flagellants' attainments are superior to our own. . . . It seems as if man has never done exploits for God without first denying himself."

(Sketch Book)

E

Thus the pages fell into the binders, dripping with aversion. David Brainerd's self-sadism was intolerable, insufferably at odds with the cherished complacency of an atomic age. Weariness and dejection finally stopped my pen. . . .

With sleep came an horror of great darkness. My own body seemed diseased, my own hopes broken off. I stirred about in great distress—"How shall I do?" A Voice that needeth not words replied, "Do you think you could have done as well as David?" And my heart cried, "O God! I could never have borne it!"

So I awoke from my dreams, recovered from the bane of Ease in Zion, and, selecting David Brainerd as an example of those who spoke in the Name of the Lord through suffering affliction, hung his sepia portrait on the study walls.　　　(Sketch Book)

OW MANY WORDS THESE DAYS ARE crowding themselves into the dictionary, like Forty-niners (1900 class) trying to get into California! It seems impertinent to suggest another. But, unable at this late date to find a good generic term for men who scourge themselves, or endure scourging for the Kingdom's sake, it seems necessary. Either that, or an old term must be distended. Suppose we distend. Let us try that ancient word "flagellant." That does it! David Brainerd, Colonial Flagellant! "Flagellant on Horseback!"

To be sure, the word is dated. It puts the glass upon those melancholy back-lashers who "flourished" [sic!] throughout Europe in the thirteenth and fourteenth centuries—that company of queer ones who, to divert divine wrath from an evil age, castigated *themselves!* In the show window of history you may see them in large, disorderly bands, bearing knotted scourges, loaded with lead, arms and shoulders bare. The whip is lifted. Is he actually going to ply it to his own back? Butterflies fill your stomach. The thongs whistle down. There is the sickening-sweet sound of leather and metal falling on quivering flesh: spurts of blood. "How revolting!"

* * *

The convenient way for disposing of an abhorrent thing is to wrap it in a phrase of contempt. So the word "flagellant" offers itself as a label, convenient not only for classifying the Fools of

67

Perugia, but also any of that entire company which through the Christian centuries has stood on the fringes "clothed in white." Flagellants are all of a kind, though their outward appearance varies greatly. Sometimes self-immolation is concealed. It is only when the outer garments are rent that spectators cry, "Behold! he had sackcloth within upon his flesh" (II Kings 6:30). Sometimes the scourging is too subtle for human sight—a perpetual self-effacement that could wish itself "accursed from Christ" for the brethren (Romans 9:3).

* * *

So, we venture to denominate Brainerd a "flagellant." It is sophistry to object to this usage on the ground that "the flagellant was a mere exhibitionist." That label was attached by Rome, the master exhibitionist of the ages. Rome opposed the flagellants not because they were "mere exhibitionists," but because they affirmed the superiority of true penance over sacraments and priestly ministrations.

But this book is not a brief for the flagellants. It simply appropriates the ancient epithet, and, as Oliver Wendell Holmes suggested, brings this verbal relic forward again "over a new route, by a new and express train of associations."

* * *

To a comfortable Zion, Mr. Flagellant is a public nuisance, if not a menace. The slow of heart admire his achievements, but—they say—"there was no need of his doing things the hard way. The same result could have been gotten without—well, without so much fuss about it." And history replies, "Oh, yes? meaning whom for example?" For history stubbornly contends that the flagellant alone is the agent who causes earth to bring forth her fruits. And the hiding of power in David Brainerd was that set of the soul which came upon him in 1743, through which self-effacement was put upon his inward parts and written on his heart.

The burden of this chapter is to set forth those things in order, through which Brainerd became a flagellant. There were several converging causes, but the occasion was his expulsion from Yale; and the time of this change was April 20, 1742, his twenty-fourth birthday.

* * *

Herewith are listed, in order, the causes.

There was his frail body, passed down from Hezekiah, his tubercular father, and further frayed by his own ascetic stresses in living. You may follow this pathetic story from the month of August, 1740, when he began to spit blood from overstudy in Yale, to those dark hours just before he died, when, as Edwards shockingly reports, "his distemper preyed on his vitals in an extraordinary manner . . . a constant discharge of purulent matter in great quantities." Of the long anguish he endured, chained to a broken body, more must be said as this narrative unfolds.

There was also a congenital dejection, no doubt inflamed by constant sickness. Edwards remarks, "He was by constitution and temper prone to melancholy and dejection of spirit." This fathomless gloom created self-doubt and self-abasement. Such things are not always the specifications of a flagellant. We have encountered flagellants who seemed vulgarly healthy and incurably optimistic.

The chief cause of his final commitment to self-effacement was that zeal for the King's house which ate him up: a zeal which seemed always to be marked by two factors—utter devotion to God, and, therefore, utter devotion to man:

O that I could be as busy for Christ as the angels. . . . I want nothing else, but that Christ should reign. I feel as if my all was lost, and I was undone if poor heathen may not be converted.   (Memoirs)

Therefore, he was willing to make sackcloth also his garment, and become a ditty for the drunkards (Psalm 69:7-12).

But the *occasion,* the fiery furnace which fused the disparate *causes* into the flagellant temper, was Brainerd's expulsion from Yale. It is difficult to imagine literature excelling the bitter-sweet of his *Memoirs,* wherein his soul, wounded by disgrace, limped like a stricken thing over the floor of hell. At first, he hoped the Yale governors might be persuaded to temper the severity of his punishment. Many direct appeals were made in his behalf by prominent men and organizations, such as Aaron Burr,* Ebenezer Pemberton, and the Ministerial Association of Hartford, Connecticut.

"The penalty you have inflicted is out of keeping with the insignificance of the offense. You will ruin the young minister's entire life," was the burden of these protests.

But the Yale governors stiffly repulsed every appeal. In fact, there is a tradition that Princeton originated from public disgust over Yale's treatment of Brainerd.

*   *   *

Brainerd himself, a humble suppliant, rode into the Yale campus several times during 1742. The pale anguish of the boy became such an annoyance to Rector Clap that orders were issued

---

* Rev. Aaron Burr is not to be confused with his son, Aaron Burr, unhappy adventurer in amatory quests and slayer of Alexander Hamilton.

for Brainerd's arrest. It seems incredible, when we read the accounts of how Brainerd, fearing arrest, came to New Haven furtively and hid out nights on the farms!

* * *

We now record how causes and occasion merged as of the twentieth day of April, 1742, and how our subject was transmuted into a flagellant; how coming to abhor himself, utterly to die to self, he committed his way to the will of God, come what may.

Immediately after Brainerd's expulsion from Yale, Jedediah Mills sought out the stricken lad in his New Haven quarters.

"David, Mrs. Mills and I would like to have you live with us in the manse. You may continue your studies for the ministry under my direction. You shall have the prophet's chamber! And here is a book we've just purchased for you to help you in your studies."

Mills pressed into Brainerd's hand a bulky, new copy of a Hebrew lexicon. That very book may be seen today in the library of Princeton University. . . . It seemed reasonable to conclude that Edwards, when he died in 1758, must have passed the volume to the college. A letter from the Department of Rare Books confirmed this supposition, and in November, 1948, we made a special pilgrimage to Princeton to examine the valuable relic.

* * *

During the next four months Brainerd applied himself with consuming zeal to his studies under Jedediah Mills; so much so indeed that when he moved from the Mills parsonage at the end of that time, he was esteemed "sufficiently advanced to be licensed to preach." But during these studies, he frequently saddled his horse and rode considerable distances to counsel with "dear ministers" in Connecticut towns and villages—Cook at Stratford, Graham at Southbury, Bellamy at Bethlehem.*

And always, on these interstudy rides, Brainerd rode in anguish of soul. Rode and wept around Turkey Hills. Rode in confusion through Hebron and Lebanon. Cried out repeatedly, "O Death, Death! my friend! hasten and deliver me!" In feverish sorrow he returned to his room and studied, until his candle vied with dawn. Then he rode again the next day.

You may note how characteristics typical to a flagellant developed with his anguish. . . . A ghastly devotion to the service of God appeared. As he waxed low in spirit, he "was made to possess the sins of his youth." By that he meant chiefly his party spirit, which brought on the Yale disgrace. This filled him with a pleasing pain: and the pleasing pain made his soul press after God. This sweet sorrow in turn often brought him to his knees in the cold forest of Connecticut, sometimes before sunrise, sometimes long after twilight. In these gloomy trysts, as he knelt in the cold wind, his whole body became wet with perspiration. You think, "Terrible exposure for a sick man!" He would have replied, "Why not? Christ sweat blood for me!"

Thus his anguish provided the soil in which dreadful effacement lodged and grew. When he prayed, he noted the absence of the prayer-sweetness he once knew. But he kept on praying even when he felt amazingly deserted. And hereupon the iron

---

* Many of the men mentioned in the *Memoirs* were of high excellence; Joseph Bellamy, for instance. Brainerd called him his "very dear friend." He was two years younger than Brainerd; born on a farm near Wallingford. From a child, his great mental powers were apparent. He entered Yale at sixteen, studied theology for two years with Edwards, and was licensed to preach at eighteen. At nineteen he accepted the pastorate at Bethlehem, and served until his death, 1790, fifty-two years later. Bellamy's books were religious best sellers in his day.

thinking began which was later to keep him in the saddle though burning with fever, "and nothing came from him but blood." He must ride! He esteemed himself utterly mean and vile. Therefore let God do with him as He wished. He ought to carry on for God in distresses and death of any sort! He was unworthy of any favor from God. Therefore, *he could think of undergoing the greatest sufferings for Christ with pleasure!*

* * *

The missionary dreams "which the Yale affair had damped," slowly began to reappear. His heart burned anew for the salvation of great numbers of the heathen: burned anew with love for God. He thereupon perceived that when his heart was hot for God and for man, he could bear with indifference any suffering. All of his anguish had been Christ's School to teach him this valuable lesson: he must never lose the benefits of anguish. If greater sufferings were yet to come, he would welcome them. Yes, he would even court sufferings.

Victory began to appear in his whole field of battle, even with respect to his enemies—

Spent an hour in prayer with the most tender affection towards mankind. I longed that my enemies might be eternally happy. It seemed refreshing to think of meeting them in heaven.　　　(Memoirs)

* * *

We are now ready to record the birth of a flagellant. On the night of April 20, 1742, his twenty-fourth birthday, he entered his room at the Mills residence. For some time he knelt, buried his face in his hands and wept. Of a sudden his grief crystallized. He took his quill and wrote:

"I WANT TO WEAR MY LIFE OUT IN HIS SERVICE AND FOR
HIS GLORY."   (Memoirs)

*   *   *

Thus his twenty-fourth birthday may be viewed as the time
when he became a confirmed and relentless flagellant. A few
entries from the *Memoirs* are quoted at random, selected to exhibit his extreme self-immolation. For instance, our age puts
a premium on a modicum of zest and youthful jollity.

To him such things were anathema. He would have none of them!
Think of the life of Christ, and when you find He was pleased with
jesting and merriment, you may indulge them yourself.

In keeping with this attitude, we find him praying, March 14,
1744, as he closed his Kaunaumeek pastorate:

"I beseech Thee, God, that I might not be too much pleased and
amused with dear friends and acquaintances one place and another." (And
the chiefest of these dear friends was Jerusha!)

As a matter of fact, he was grateful for gloom—it kept him
humble and resigned.

He had sweet joy in the thought of hardship, even death itself. Distresses in Christian service were blessings. So he prayed that many distresses might alight upon him—*and upon his dear brother John!*

The life of a true Christian, therefore, in Brainerd's view, was
an unbroken process of consuming oneself for the glory of God.
The travail incident thereto is life's true pleasure! When he lay
dying he advised two young ministers: "Frequently engage in
secret fasting. It is a great comfort. I would not mention this
were I not a dying person."

His flagellant temper drove him to grisly doctrinal positions:

True religion has scant place in it for rejoicing; even rejoicing over
salvation by grace. True religion was fundamentally known by an abasing

sense of unworthiness. It was of heresy for a Christian to teach or think that Christ died for him *personally;* no man was worth *that!*

How far he went with that doctrine, so strange to our age, may be seen in a heated argument he had with an eminent Boston minister after his fatal hemorrhage of June, 1747. Gasping for breath, he said:

That kind of faith (Christ died for me personally) wholly left out the essence of saving belief; it had nothing of God in it; nothing above nature, nor indeed above the power of devils; all who had such faith, and no better, though they might have it to never so high a degree, would surely perish.

His last weeks at Northampton were often marked by an almost petulant review of the "dangerous doctrine, 'Christ died for me personally,'" being scattered by "men of a recent dogma."

He was also positive that the motivation for a Christian's getting to heaven was not his personal hope of advance. The reason for getting to heaven was to glorify God, and that consideration only should animate the mind.

* * *

We may look upon these alarming views with some degree of extenuation when we remember they were simply flagellantism raised to the nth power. There was no place in his scheme of praxis or principle for self. Self must be entirely blotted out.

Our age, when it desires to canonize a man, while at the same time condemning his philosophy, has a ready aphorism: "Men are often better than their theology." This is a good screed with which to fend off the blows of an awakened conscience. But what shall be done with this sentence:

"They overcame him by the blood of the Lamb, and by the word of their testimony; and *they loved not their lives unto the death"?—Revelation 12:11.*

* * *

Of the multitude whose wills have been assaulted by the *Memoirs,* some have yielded completely, some in part, and some— *have protested too much!*

From the moment of Brainerd's twenty-fourth birthday, he became a living sacrifice, body and soul; holy, totally expendable, acceptable to God. From that hour his set face never relaxed! His furious devotion knew no rest until that morning when as he lay dying, Jonathan Edwards, with his arm about his sorrowing daughter, said:

"Look, Jerusha! he is smiling! He has been welcomed by the glorious assembly into the upper world."

VIII

Flagellant Refined and Approved

(LICENSED JULY 29, 1742—COMMISSIONED NOVEMBER 25, 1742)

In which we follow with unequal step the plan of God wherein He employed disappointments to refine a brokenhearted boy: then, so fast as the lad obeyed the heavenly vision, moved men in authority to load him with heavenly honors. This has always been the favorite course with the Ancient of Days. "Men become good; God maketh them great."

"July 29, 1742. It was sweet to feel myself in favor again."

"The Lord's Day, December 12, 1742. This has been a sweet Sabbath to me, and blessed be God, I have reason to think my religion is becoming more spiritual by means of my late outward conflicts. Amen! May I always be willing that God should use His own methods with me."   (Memoirs)

IN CONNECTION WITH HIS TOTAL disposal to the service of Heaven, certain effects are immediately evident. Compare his decision of April 20—"I want to wear my life out in His service and for His glory"—with the entry of May 1—"Had a profitable week in my studies."

This subtle change mantled his entire outlook. There was the matter of his rides abroad between study periods. These he continued, traveling astonishing distances. For example, May 10, ten miles each way to New Haven; May 11, forty miles to Wethersfield; May 13, fifteen miles to Hartford. Formerly he "rode in confusion all the way." Now his "desires ascended unto God as he traveled."

It is true that he still felt from time to time the burden of his disgrace; but now he was able to rise above it. July 3, for instance:

When the remembrance of his disgrace damped him, he immediately turned to the Rock that was higher than himself.

*   *   *

The summer wore on, and the time approached for him to meet the Presbyterian ministers who were to examine him with respect to licensing him to preach the gospel. Accordingly, in July he rode south through the mountains of western Connecticut towards Danbury, where the ministers were to hold their council.

He was secretly troubled over the attitude the brethren might take toward recognizing a man who had been expelled from college.

79

En route, he stopped at Bethlehem to visit with Mr. Bellamy; heard him preach July 11. Mr. Bellamy said at the noon meal, "Mr. Brainerd, after your license to preach, we would like to have you live with us until you begin your ministry."

So, Brainerd reasoned, "the brilliant Mr. Bellamy and his devoted young wife held no aversion toward him! That made him praise God."

July 28, he rode into Danbury. . . . When the motion was made the next day to license him, he could hardly believe his senses. Instead of misgivings, the brethren seemed delighted with him. . . . Suppose we let him tell his own story:

I was examined by the Association met at Danbury as to my learning, and also my experience in religion, and received from them a license to preach the gospel of Christ. Afterwards felt much devoted to God. . . . Went to bed resolved to live devoted to God all my days.

*   *   *

Now that he was licensed to preach, it is fascinating to trace the influences which gradually turned his heart to Indian missions as the particular field for his ministerial service; to note the causes that led him to gird himself with a towel and serve a marginal race.

To be sure, Brainerd's writings make it clear that he had always been interested in Red Men. His leadings in this direction were enlarged by the very atmosphere he breathed, Indian missions being uppermost in Colonial thinking.

They wrote missions into their colony charters, and reaffirmed missions in their young schools of learning. One chief reason that led to the founding of the Plymouth and Boston Colonies was the desire to Christianize the Indians. . . . This purpose may be seen today in the seal of the Commonwealth of Massachusetts,

Packet 5

INDIAN STUDIES

The Indian—what shall we say of him?

If one happens to be a person in the mold of David Brainerd, one will affirm that Mr. Indian is as deeply loved by the Eternal of Days as anyone listed in *Who's Who*; and that, as such, Mr. Indian, too, is worthy of Greater Love's Great Sacrifice (John 15:13).

*Photos by Milton Snow
for Navaho Service
Window Rock, Arizona*

SILVERSMITH OF THE
PAINTED DESERT

PROUD, VALIANT SERVICEMAN

MAIDEN OF THE PAINTED
DESERT

Navaho Indians are not
allowed to vote, although
they are citizens and
3,600 men and women served
in the armed forces.

which motto has so frequently bannered the missionary enter-
prise—"Come over and help us." *

During student days Brainerd learned of a resolution voted by
the Yale Board of Trustees at the first meeting:

"To plant and under ye Divine blessing to propagate in this Wilderness
the blessed Reformed Protestant Religion in ye purity of its Order and
Worship not only to their posterity but also to the barbarous nations."

*   *   *

From earliest times, too, the women of the Colonies devoted
the mother that was in them to missionary societies and missionary
studies; and as a result, marked their minds with a peculiar
character. It is no surprise therefore to find that their sons and
daughters did not view missionary labors as sacrificial or bemean-
ing, but rather, as distinctive.

An example of a man of brilliant gifts, a son of one of the
best homes, deciding upon missions as a career, was John Sergeant.
Brainerd, during his Yale days, absorbed every scrap of information about the "former student who was now the famous worker
among the Housatonic Indians—John Sergeant."

The name of Sergeant became fixed in Brainerd's roster of
Christian heroes. He knew how John's father, Jonathan, was
one of the congregation which moved to New Jersey and founded
Newark, 1666, where John was born, 1710. How John as a boy
accidentally mutilated his left hand with a keen scythe. How
his folks had said, "He is not fit for farm duties; we'll make
a preacher out of him."

He never tired of recalling how this handicapped boy became
valedictorian of Yale's class of 1729. How the young graduate
was sought after by strong churches: how he replied, "I'd rather

* Arthur Cushman McGiffert, *Jonathan Edwards.* Harper and Brothers, 1932.

F

be employed as a missionary to the Indians, if any door should open for it, than accept a call any English parish might give."

Brainerd actually wept over the outcome of this declaration. Two clergymen representing the Society for the Propagation of the Gospel in New England went to Boston and challenged Sergeant:

"We heard of what you said. The door is open, Mr. Sergeant!"

He laughed with joy over Sergeant's reply:

"I was just wondering how long it would take you to get here!"

*   *   *

Yes, Sergeant's life was to Brainerd one of Faith's sweetest narratives. He thought of Sergeant's devotion when he went to work among the Indians in 1735: "He became beloved by them as their father and best friend"; he mastered the Indian tongues to such a degree that an old brave said,

"Him speak better Indian than us!"

He was familiar with the unique work Sergeant conducted on his six-mile square tract of land at Stockbridge, Massachusetts. How he labored with deathless zeal for the salvation of the Indians, then with equal zeal labored to educate the Indians for practical living. Sergeant unknowingly shaped Brainerd's future work at Cranberry by his ringing declaration,

"I am going to provide vocational guidance for every Indian boy and girl."

*   *   *

And of course there was another influence that wedded his soul to Indian missions. Her name? Well, you shall never, throughout this story, be permitted to forget her—Miss Jerusha Edwards.

Would Brainerd ever forget that first time he saw her, when she rode down from Northampton to the Yale commencement of 1741?

Edwards was always riding down to New Haven. After one of these trips, July 28, 1727, he rode back with Miss Sarah Pierrepont—pardon, Mrs. Jonathan Edwards! daughter of one of Yale's founders. . . .

In 1741, when Edwards rode down to Yale to deliver the baccalaureate sermon, as mentioned in a previous chapter, he was accompanied by one of his own daughters, Jerusha, who was her beautiful mother Sarah all over again!

Jerusha and David did not formally *meet* that day, but bless me, they did *see* each other! . . . Mr. Edwards was so eloquent when he gave the baccalaureate sermon. So witty, too. Said there were both good and bad features in revivals: "just like Solomon's ships: when they brought gold and silver and pearls, they also brought apes and peacocks." He *would* never forget that!

And he *could* never forget Miss Jerusha, the slender young beauty of twelve! She was a relative of the notable Indian missionary Mr. Sergeant. She also had missionary leadings. It all added up.

* * *

When Brainerd finally did meet Jerusha, and began calling at the Northampton parsonage (a matter which Edwards almost succeeded in editing out of the *Account*), there came a memorable afternoon in October, 1743. As the young couple talked, he was not surprised to hear her say that she too had decided to become an Indian missionary, and—

"Father is giving me a course of study on 'The Missionary's Wife.'"

When Brainerd rode away from Northampton that day, he galloped—and fast! It was adding up, indeed!

* * *

The *Memoirs* disclose how Brainerd's heart irrevocably turned to the Indians:

O that God would bring in great numbers of the Indians to Christ, *and use me in the effecting of it.* . . . I have no desire for the conversion of the Indians that I might receive honor from the world . . . I am weaned from the world, willing to be despised. . . .

And then you witness the crisis in his thinking:

"DEAR FATHER, EMPLOY ME IN THAT WORK!"

* * *

The day following the meeting of the Presbytery at Danbury, he rode north on a road skirting the west side of Connecticut. He was

in a most ecstatic state of soul . . . He panted for a complete restoration in him of the image of his Saviour . . . he had lost hope in a great measure of being sent to the heathen afar off. . . .

He now hoped that God would disclose a field for him among the wigwams of the Colonies. But since he did not as yet have a formal appointment, he would at least begin at Jerusalem.

Almost mechanically, he turned his horse towards the Waramaug Valley, just south of Waramaug Lake, nestling at the west base of the Above All Mountain.*

There in the valley a band of Indians lived in a wigwam village. He rode through Kent and into the village. His heart

---

* No portion of the United States deserves a Sir Walter Scott more than the Above All Mountain area, distinguished, as it is, by sheer beauty and historic richness. At least "seventeen goodly cedars" like Bellamy and Finney were nourished on its slopes. We would gladly make other pilgrimages there! (See *Man of Like Passions.*)

burned with love as he preached to them through an Indian interpreter.

"Some cried out in distress; all were greatly concerned. . . ."

He remembered what Mr. Sergeant had repeatedly written: "We must not fail to follow our soul-winning with secular instruction." So

"he hired an English woman [at his own charges!] to keep a kind of school among them before he rode on."

*   *   *

Day by day as he rode the Connecticut trails, Indian peoples became dearer to him. Often he stopped in the woodlands to pray, "O God, open a way for me."

Your heart is touched as you watch this non-commissioned boy. You think, "If there ever was a man worthy of being made an Indian missionary, it was David Brainerd." But—*God saw that before you did!*

*   *   *

The denouement came with dramatic power. On the nineteenth day of November a horseman from New York City, who had been tracking Brainerd for days, caught up with him in New Haven. He was a messenger from Rev. Ebenezer Pemberton, "Secretary of the Correspondents in New York, New Jersey and Pennsylvania of the *Society in Scotland for the Propagation of Christian Knowledge*"! Dear me! may I never be obliged to ask a linotypist to tap that out again. In the rest of this book, can we not refer to this Society as "the SSPCK"?

The messenger said, "Mr. Brainerd, Mr. Pemberton wants you to report in New York at your earliest convenience, to discuss

the possibility of your being commissioned to work among the
Indians."

*   *   *

That night Brainerd confided some glowing lines to the
Memoirs:

This seems too good to be true! . . . it exceeds my utmost hopes! . . .
I am mightily flustered!

To the messenger he said: "Could you wait a few hours? I'd
like to ride back to New York with you! But, first, I'd like to
confer with dear ministerial friends, and have them pray with
me for guidance!"

What a charming ministerial conceit! We have never found
offense in the remark, originally intended to be offensive:

"When a dominie receives a call to a work upon which his heart is
set, he says to his wife, 'You pray, Dear; and I'll start packing.' "

*   *   *

A week later, November 25, 1742, at Woodbridge, New Jersey, Brainerd was commissioned an Indian Missionary by the
SSPCK.

IX

The Long Ride Begins

(MARCH 24, 1743)

*Herewith the story of a ride through New England
blizzards in which our subject, prior to the departure
for his station, designed to bid his friends farewell.
But this trip turned out to be a sample of the severi-
ties he would continuously encounter upon the mission field. You will sympathize with a question that
arose in his mind: "Should I go on with this work,
or accept a comfortable pastorate?"*

*There is also, herein, the record of a character crisis
without which this biography would have col-
lapsed—*

"He chose to go rather than to stay."

In one of these weeks of boot-and-saddle fare-wells, he came to the old home town. He consented to preach for his Haddam friends and acquaintances. As he sat in the pulpit chair waiting his time, that morning of January 6, 1743, he could see through the church windows heavy swirls of stinging snow, blizzard driven. There had been so much of it—and he so constantly ill. Tomorrow he must breast it again. If he went on into the Delaware wilderness, such would be his constant life.

Seated before him were his dear friends—his sister Spencer right at the front, smiling at him. Suddenly the significance of it all became clear. He arose, opened his Bible, and announced his text, Deuteronomy 8:2:

"Thy God led thee . . . in the wilderness
to prove thee . . . whether thou wouldest
keep his commandments, or no."

(Sketch Book)

$\mathcal{J}$UST AT THIS TIME, IT IS PROPER to detain the narrative, that you may no longer be denied an account of the SSPCK. This missionary society was one of the several organizations instituted by British Christians during early days to evangelize the Colonies. A careful study of the entire matter would make a worthy student-thesis. There was, for instance: "The Society for the Evangelization and Propagation of the Gospel in Foreign Parts," founded in London, 1701; "The Corporation for the Propagation of the Gospel in New England"; and the SSPCK (The Society in Scotland for the Propagation of Christian Knowledge) which was launched in the City of Edinburgh, 1709.

In the year 1740, "several distinguished ministers of the Colonies petitioned the SSPCK to do something about the deplorable and perishing state of the Indians in the Provinces of New York, New Jersey, and Pennsylvania." Among these "distinguished ministers" were Ebenezer Pemberton of New York, and Jonathan Dickinson and Aaron Burr of New Jersey.

The SSPCK promptly responded. "They made an appropriation for two missionaries and appointed Correspondents to direct and inspect the work." The Correspondents organized, elected Pemberton secretary, Burr treasurer; and shortly thereafter Azariah Horton was commissioned to labor among the Indians at Montauk on Long Island.

The Correspondents then began looking about for a second man. Aaron Burr presented the name of David Brainerd; spoke warmly of the young man's obliging humility, deep piety, fine scholarship.

"But Mr. Burr, what about his expulsion from Yale?"

"Botheration!" shouted Burr. "You gentlemen know *Rector Clap,* don't you? . . . I move we instruct our Secretary to send out a messenger, find Mr. Brainerd, get him down to New York, and offer him the second post. . . ." In the preceding chapter, we found the horseman overtaking Brainerd in New Haven.

*   *   *

On the morning of November 21, 1742, Brainerd and the messenger rode southward by way of "the rut through the wilderness," now affectionately known as "The Boston Post Road." They wallowed through miles of slush and deluges of ice water.

"Looks like a hard winter is coming," said the messenger.

Deep snow covered the city of New York, on the southern tip of Manhattan Island, when they reached there November 23. A man's first time in New York has always been a climactic experience, a staple item for newsmen, so we'll ask Brainerd how he likes the city:

"I'm confused with this noise and tumult. I desire to shortly finish my business here and begin my missionary labors."

Shades of Amsterdam! and there was not as yet a single Yellow Taxi or Fifth Avenue Bus!

*   *   *

The meeting of the SSPCK, November 24, was held in the home of Pemberton on Cortlandt Street, somewhere just south of the present City Hall Park—if that helps you any. Brainerd was examined of his Christian experiences, and his acquaintance with divinity and other studies in order to his improvement in that important affair of evangelizing the heathen. . . . He was then forced to go and preach to a considerable assembly before some grave and learned ministers, but felt a pressure from a sense of his ignorance and unfitness. . . .

The learned ministers, too, "felt a pressure," but of an entirely different sort. They were captivated by the young preacher; his zeal for God, his humility, his downright goodness. There was no need for further examination.

*　*　*

The colonists were fascinated with the reports brought back by soldiers, scientists, and travelers in northeastern Pennsylvania; "it was a land of grandeur, riches, and primeval beauty." Men were dreaming of settling the wilderness. Of particular interest to the SSPCK, however, were the thousands of unevangelized Indians residing in the territory, particularly in the rugged terrain lying between the Susquehanna and Delaware Rivers. It was a challenging opportunity. The Commissioners had decided to send a missionary just as soon as possible. . . . Therefore, on that historic day, "they commissioned Mr. Brainerd to labor among the Pennsylvania Indians living near the Forks of the Delaware River, and the Indians living along the Susquehanna River."

When the motion was presented, Gilbert Tennent walked to the window and regarded the mounting snowdrifts.

"This is no time to start for the Forks of the Delaware," he said. "It is going to be a severe winter. A man riding the wilderness would perish. I suggest Mr. Brainerd defer starting until late March, and meet with us then for final conference. In the meantime, he can adjust his personal affairs, bid his friends farewell, and spend some time at East Hampton and Montauk, Long Island, conferring with Mr. Horton." * This was wise counsel, and the matter was so arranged.

That night the delighted boy wrote in his *Memoirs:*

Spent much of the evening alone . . . felt myself infinitely indebted to those people, and longed that God would reward them with the rewards of His grace.

*   *   *

Inasmuch as his time was practically his own until March, he set out in the bitter weather next day, Connecticut-bound, to bid farewell to his ministerial friends,

supposing it likely, since he was going to a field so remote, they should not meet again until they came to that eternal world.

One of the "adjustments in his personal affairs" had to do with his own property, likely the farm at Durham Center, and his portion of the Haddam homestead. Edwards' account of this is excellent:

Expecting to spend the remainder of his life among the Indians, he sold his patrimony, thinking he would have no further occasion for it, though afterwards, as he told me, he found himself mistaken. He set himself to think which way he might spend it to do more good; and then, being at the charge of educating a young man for the ministry, he fixed on him—and entered him in Yale! Brainerd continued to be at the charge of this boy's education from year to year, and got him to his third year in college before he, Brainerd, died.

*   *   *

The record of his Farewell Ride during the next few months is too intricate for extended detail. But you must remember, so far as weather is concerned, it was like four months in Siberia. You see him floundering day after day through snowdrifts and

* Within a year ill health forced Horton to resign.

bitter cold; through towns and villages—Derby, Ripton, New Haven, Brantford! Killingsworth, Winthrop, Deep River, Haddam! Norwich, Lebanon, Canterbury, Kent!

At Bethlehem, he conferred with an old trapper in Pastor Bellamy's congregation. This man had often journeyed far west— "knew it like a book."

"If you're going to the Delaware River," he said, "you do not need to start from Princeton and cross the lowlands; just go westward over Connecticut, swim the Hudson, then straight across the highlands to Port Jervis, and down the Delaware to the water gap." This advice Brainerd followed a year later.

* * *

For the present, on his farewell journey, he had ahead of him weeks of hard riding and heavy winter weather.

Sometimes he became so weary he seemed enclosed in hell itself; but, sometimes in the home of a friend, there was a sweet melting and a remarkable sense of divine things. . . . Sometimes with a number of friends, he found a retired place in the woods, and knelt down in the snow. . . . At intervals the sun shone gloriously over the winter wonderland. On such days he rode extra far; rode until darkness came and bitter cold; thereafter he was under the power of melancholy; in such anguish he could not eat. Sometimes he was bed-ridden for several days. And then he felt himself unworthy to look a Delaware Indian in the face.

* * *

By the end of January this rigorous living had beaten him to the buff. The time came to start for the visit to Long Island, and afterwards the March meeting of the SSPCK in New York. Wearily he rode down to East Lyme to board a Long Island ferry. A vicious blizzard blew during the entire fifty miles. Suddenly his human nature cried out within him, "This will be my life in

the Delaware wilderness . . . can I endure it? . . . should I not
turn back? O God, it would be far less difficult to lie down in
the grave."

For some time the snow swirled about him, the horse plodded
on in the storm. Suddenly he cried out,

"O GOD, I CHOOSE TO GO RATHER THAN TO STAY!"

*   *   *

The Long Island ferryboat was two days off schedule by reason
of masses of ice in the Sound. There was nothing for him to do
but to wait in the draughty, unheated ferry building; but his decision to carry on, braced his endurance. When he reached East
Hampton, he was desperately ill for ten days, "only half alive."
But Tuesday, February 16, "his weariness had so much disappeared, his soul arose above the deep waters into which it had so
lately sunk."

As soon as he could get about, winter though it was, he plunged
into a program of pastoral labors—visitation, preaching, and teaching. He conferred with the missionary, Mr. Horton; rode sixteen
muddy miles to preach for the savages at Montauk, "sensed the
terrible barriers Satan set against gospel preaching among the
Indians."

But—he had chosen to go!

*   *   *

The church at East Hampton was immediately enamored of
Brainerd, desired to have him for their pastor. It was a modish
community then, just as it is today, with its Little Theatre and
summer drama. Jonathan Edwards described it in language superlative for him:

One of the fairest, pleasantest towns on the whole Island . . . the church parish was one of the largest and most wealthy. They wanted Brainerd for their pastor. . . . Even after he was settled on the mission field, they continued for a long time in an earnest pursuit of what they desired.

Several years later, when Brainerd lay dying, Edwards asked: "Why did you refuse to take that pastorate?"

Brainerd answered: "I am an Indian missionary: and I chose to go on with that business."

*   *   *

When it came time to leave Long Island and go to New York City, the very thought of departure from the church "gave him an inward deadness." He could scarcely stand. But his course of life, like Enoch's, was not to please himself; he must walk with God.

For an hour and a half he was sweetly assisted to insist on a closer walk with God, as his final message.

*   *   *

The commissioners appeared rather brusque when they met with him, March 16, at Woodbridge, New Jersey. It seemed as if "he was speedily dismissed by them." In a most surprising way they told him he was not to go to the Forks of the Delaware: he was instead to proceed to Kaunaumeek in the Province of New York.*

*   *   *

Why such a change in plans? The reasons were sound. At that time there was such a critical land squabble on the Delaware

* Pronounced "Kaw-naw-meek," no accent.

between savage and settler that it was deemed untimely to open the mission. John Sergeant wrote the SSPCK suggesting that Brainerd fill in a year, while the trouble was abating,

". . . working among some scattered Indians at Kaunaumeek. At the same time he could give Brainerd lessons in the native languages."

Nevertheless, the changed plans were disappointing. Brainerd, on his recent journey, had told everybody he was going to the Delaware. . . . But, after all, he was an Indian missionary; *where* he labored was not important.

How irrevocable this committal was may be seen in a subsequent *Memoir* entry:

He felt disconsolate. . . . But, no other labor appealed to him: he had no freedom in the thought of any other business in life.

*   *   *

At 9:00 a.m., March 25, 1743, Brainerd left New York City, riding northward towards Kaunaumeek. Despondency sat heavily upon him during the fifty miles of that first day. He could see nothing ahead save discomfort, suffering—and death.

BUT, HE HAD CHOSEN TO GO RATHER THAN TO STAY.

Packet 6

INDIAN STUDIES, Continued

Photo by Milton Snow, for Navaho Service

So you think mistreatment of the American Indian no longer continues?

Well, remember that thirty-six hundred "proud, valiant Navahos" served in our armed forces—when we needed them. But today, 1950, most of the Navaho families are sick, hungry, badly housed. When one comes upon the grave of a Navaho child in the desert, its body unburied, its "pathetic little possessions heaped upon it," he cannot help thinking of America's broken covenants respecting schools, hospitals, and soldier allotments.

PESSIMISM

In the 1868 treaty, the United States guaranteed to the Navahos a teacher and classroom for every 30 children, a promise never kept. Today, there are 14,000 Navaho children without schools.

"JESUS' LITTLE LAMBS"

Most Navahos are sick, hungry, and badly housed. Their one-room hogans are windowless, unsanitary, uncomfortable, and overcrowded. Water must be hauled many miles. Few families have furniture, but sleep, eat, and live on the dirt floor, on which everyone spits. There is 8½ times as much T.B. as in the United States generally. Infant mortality is appalling. There are only 365 hospital beds and 182 T.B. beds for 55,000 Indians. There is no public health education—no public health service— there are no field nurses.

Photos by the Stokelys of Gadtiahi

GRAVE OF A NAVAHO CHILD

The little body lies unburied upon the ground . . . with his few possessions. "Offended childhood and millstones for nations."

X

Lo! the Poor Indian

(1492-1950)

In which we face the treatment accorded the North American Indian from the time early settlers fell first upon their knees, then upon the aborigines, to the latest grandiose gesture, wherein the government helicoptered some groceries to a people it had helped to starve. . . . We are also to note the sharply contrasting procedure of Heaven which assigns its noblest servants to marginal peoples.

"When he saw the multitudes, he was moved with compassion on them, because they fainted, and were scattered abroad, as sheep having no shepherd. Then saith he unto his disciples, The harvest truly is plenteous, but the labourers are few; pray ye therefore the Lord of the harvest, that he will send forth labourers into his harvest."—*Matthew 9:36-38.*

"I can think myself of undergoing the greatest suffering in the cause of Christ with pleasure, that I might serve for Him among the Indians."

(Memoirs)

KNOWING HIS DECISION NO LONGER allowed him to count his life as dear unto himself, Brainerd rode forth that day in March, 1743, to devote his pathetically few remaining months to the North American Indian. This naturally is unintelligible to Mr. Worldly Wise —"It's foolish for that boy, who moved with ease among college presidents, to throw away his life! literally to bury himself among savages in the wilderness! Just no sense to it!"

No sense to it—unless you too have heard a Voice; a Voice one never forgets, saying, "Whom shall I send, and who will go for Me?" Then one understands how a man can lay down his life for—the Indian!

* * *

The Indian! What shall we say of him?

The fabulist poses him beside his painty ingleside, wigwam, wickiup, hogan, or pueblo, as the Dream Boy of a New World. But the realist observes that he has a type of male selfishness not to be outdone, his theme song apparently being, "Let the women do the work." The pioneer views him as an obstructionist who "hasn't done a thing with the land for a thousand years, and is set on seeing nobody else does." (Just think of that uranium, oil, coal, going to waste on the Painted Desert!) The sentimentalist draws tears by the haunting strains of "Lo! the poor Indian."

Visit Mr. Indian on Yavapai during his Spring awakening ceremony. You can scarcely bear the odor of the dead cow from which his festival steaks are cut. But, as an offset to the whirr of the

ankle-bound snake rattles, you remember that boys from the
wickiups have served in the highest places in our Federal Government.

* * *

"What will I do with him?" you cry.

You think of him Smoki-dancing his frantic rain prayer, with
a bunch of snakes, like earth worms, hanging out of his mouth.
Then you know, "He's quite a bit of no good!" This is the final
judgment—until someone beside you whispers:

"Take it easy! Those 'Indians' are really white businessmen
from Prescott, doing an Arizona Chamber of Commerce turn."

Your adverse judgment against Mr. Indian promptly blows up
in your face: "Why! white men are as bad as Indians!"

That's just about the way it stands in the end. A man from
Mars could write as devastating a case against gentlemen from
Boston's Back Bay, as he could against the Diggers of Inyo
Country.

But, if one happens to be a person in the mold of David Brainerd, he can affirm that Mr. Indian is as deeply loved by the Eternal
of Days as anyone listed in *Who's Who.* Mr. Indian has the same
abysmal faults; but he has also the same vaulting possibilities as
Mr. White Man. As such, Mr. Indian, too, is worthy of Greater
Love's Great Sacrifice (John 15:13). If one has Brainerd's
"frame," he understands that when a missionary, counting not his
life as dear unto himself, rides out into the wilderness seeking
Indians, the angels, who seem to be delightfully color blind in
the matter of race pigments, promptly fill heaven with the
Anthems of Redemption.

Speaking of the Annals of Infamy, the treatment accorded the
North American Indian makes an embarrassing chapter.

"But what about those bestial scalping parties? that terrible page of burned homes?" We do not exculpate; we simply remind you that Mr. Indian was a roiled-up savage. Remember how white men, land hungry, mineral hungry, woman hungry—hammered him about like human pucks. One group of whites gave the Indian whisky; another group, often the same men, penalized the Indian for being disorderly. There's quite a bit of point in the old ditty about the Redskin:

> "You'll find his name in history,
>   But it forgot to say
> The White Man gave him whisky once,
>   And sent him on his way."

That is, one set of white men, the traders, gave him whisky; and another set, the politicians, "to preserve order," sent him on his way. It was the old badger game, early American.

* * *

"What became of the Indians?"

"Well, we *helped* them get away."

As an example, the Government helped the Turkeys, the Turtles, and the Wolves over to Ohio, then on to Missouri, then to Kansas. Then, we helped ourselves to Indian land! So many Indians perished in that six state trek that of the multitude which started only seven hundred and eighty males remained "to become American citizens" [sic] when the exodus reached the plains of Kansas!

* * *

"Well, that's all over," you say. Is it? Get out the records. See armed cavalrymen in 1862, with bared bayonets, drive thousands of Navahos to southern New Mexico. Remember how these displaced savages languished for months behind wooden stockades—that is, those who did not die en route as American soldiers prodded them on.

"All over," is it?

In World War II, thirty-six hundred Navaho Indians served in the armed forces. Their military record was notable. But when soldier allotments and war incomes ended in 1947, inadequate relief appropriations as of the Fall of 1948 limited direct per capita relief to $5.00 per month.* Today most of the families are sick, hungry, badly housed. A child's grave, body unburied in the desert, compels one to remember the scores of broken covenants.

When the blizzards of 1949 struck, big hearted Uncle Sam flew in some groceries for "the poor, starving Indians"!

"All over," is it?

Sixty-two thousand people out in the Painted Desert are today receiving such treatment that Red Communists find there a ready field for propaganda. Why is it that Navahos today receive $64.00 per capita of Federal benefits, while Whites receive $315.00? Why are relief food trucks, which began rumbling to the reservations as a result of the scandal of 1947, not running in 1949? Why are thousands of Indians living on bread and coffee? Why are eighty per cent of the Navahos illiterate? Why are our solemn treaties still violated, and no adequate schools provided? Why NOT ONE Government field doctor, not one field nurse? Why only one school nurse when children by the thousands are tubercular? Why five small Government hospitals—all closed?

Why, we do not know. Maybe you should write the New Mexico Association on Indian Affairs at Santa Fe.

"All over," is it?

* Report of the New Mexico Association on Indian Relief.

Since the uranium deposit agreements have been worked out,
we cannot help wondering, "Isn't it about time the Indians are
'helped' again?" We try to get our missionary friends, Edith and
Berlyn, up in Gadtiahi, to talk:

"What do you think of it?"

"We don't know. We're just watching."

* * *

"We're just watching!"

That's typical of the missionary. He is first of all and last of
all a watchman for the King. So, as Brainerd begins his long
ride, we know his main concern; he is to be a watchman constantly alerted on the walls, watching in behalf of his beloved
people. His watching will demand life-giving labors over and
above his daily hours of preaching, teaching, and visiting in the
wigwams. He will find it necessary to spend other hours instruct-
ing these simple people how to make a living, how to keep well;
of which this book will have more to say in Chapter XVI,
"Prophet in Overalls."

Brainerd's watching will also mean learning the Indian languages; "every man loves to hear the gospel in his own tongue."
That in itself is exacting labor. Indian languages and dialects
have prismatic diversity. It will be difficult for him to gain acquaintance with these dialects,

seeing his other labors and fatigues engross the whole of his time. But
he would nevertheless take considerable pains—as far as his other business
and bodily health would permit. . . . He learned to pronounce their words.

He will keep at the dialects until within a few months he will
be translating prayers for them, translating hymns for them
to sing:

They take pains and are apt in learning to sing Psalm tunes [which, dear Reader, we doubt you could do]. They become able to sing with a good degree of decency in the worship of God.

This "good degree of vocal decency," soon to come from the forests which had for aeons resounded to medicine chants, will no doubt delight the angels in glory.

*   *   *

Our Lone Rider will soon become so proficient in the dialects that he will be able to preach in them:

"They sat and listened as I preached to them three hours at a time."

And this unusual attentiveness of his congregations, he was to explain with characteristic self-deprecation:

"They listened to my low and vulgar methods of expression because they were familiar with my voice." [Shades of Demosthenes! we wish that were true even of us who address English-speaking audiences!]

*   *   *

Ah, Good Friends, we want you to appreciate this young man starting on his long ride. To be sure, you will be shocked to find that his terrible devotion will soon end his life. But you will also find this terrible devotion was the precise reason why—

HE BORE HIS GREAT COMMISSION IN HIS FACE.

XI

Kaunaumeek

(APRIL 1, 1743—APRIL 30, 1744)

*In which the Commissioners' altered direc-
tive begins to make sense. "Proceed to Kaunaumeek," they said; "not to the Forks of the
Delaware." Brainerd soon realized that this apparently unimportant station in the Province of
New York was in fact a Boot School for missionaries.*

We resent the opinion of certain writers who ad-judge John Sergeant as "stupid." "Him plenty smart," said the Indians. And certain graces possessed by Mark Hopkins appear to have reached him in a genealogical knight move from his ancestor—John Sergeant.

"My ideal of a college," said President Garfield, at a Williams Alumni Dinner in New York City, "would be fully met by a saw log in the woods with a student at one end and Mark Hopkins at the other."

The idea was not new. Hopkins' great-grandfather, John Sergeant, sat on one end of a log in the Stock-bridge wilderness; and David Brainerd, an Indian language student, sat on the other. (Sketch Book)

LOOK AT A MAP OF NEW YORK
State and you will see that the distance from New York City to
Brainard Station, as the crow flies, is in excess of one hundred
and twenty miles. Brainard Station is to be found on the map
fourteen miles southeast of Albany on Highway 20. But a horseman does not cover that space as the crow flies. Brainerd's route
went through the mountains of Western Connecticut to Stockbridge, Massachusetts, thence northwest to Kaunaumeek (Brainard Station).

All day Thursday, Friday, and Saturday, his steed floundered
along the mountain roads, still ermined with splotches of snow.
. . . Sunday he preached for the Indians at Scaticock. Monday
the rain fell in deluges, so he was obliged to stay in Kent. Mounted
again, he rode all day Tuesday and Wednesday. Thursday evening, dog weary, he tied his horse in front of John Sergeant's
home on the Indian School grounds at Stockbridge. "He was
overwhelmed with peculiar gloom and melancholy." Scant wonder! Eight days on the road! And hard riding always made
him ill.

But the horseback hours gave him time to discern one reason,
at least, which the Commissioners had in mind when they changed
the orders. The Commissioners had said just as he was leaving:
"We want you to study the Indian languages for a year under
Mr. Sergeant at Stockbridge. You can frequently ride over to
his home for your lessons. It is only twenty miles from Kaunaumeek." (Shades of Pegasus! It would have been interesting,

107

no end, to see the gentlemen of the SSPCK frequently ride that
no-year route through virgin timber!) But he was to study under
John Sergeant, the man whose achievements had so fired his
heart when he was a Yale student; and—John Sergeant's wife was
a relative of Jerusha's! Those aspects of his Kaunaumeek sojourn
seemed to cushion his disappointment.

The Commissioners desired, furthermore, that Brainerd inspect
at close range Sergeant's program of combining evangelism and
secular instruction. . . . Yes, the affair did begin to make sense.
Kaunaumeek was to be for him a sort of missionary training
school.

*　*　*

The Sergeants were charming folks—practically newlyweds.
Mrs. Sergeant—Abigail—was a daughter of rascally old Col.
Ephraim Williams of Stockbridge, and just about as winsome as
her father was nepotic.* In the course of an evening's conversation, many points were settled upon: such matters as arrangements for Brainerd's language lessons; the necessity for the education of the Indians.

"And another thing," said Sergeant. "You will find it impossible to work among the Indians without a good interpreter. When
you are ready, I will send you John Wauwaumpequunaunt." †

Sergeant told Brainerd it would be possible for him to live
with Mr. and Mrs. Jim McGinlay at Kaunaumeek until he made
other arrangements.

---

* The reader will not begrudge this footnote. Col. Williams, a relative of Edwards',
became to him during his Stockbridge pastorate, a thorn in the flesh. "Williams (wrote
Edwards) is trying to get control of mission property, and is constantly busy with lime juice,
punch and wine."

But "Old Eph. Williams, the Lord of the Valley," had some mighty fine daughters. One
of them was associated with Williams College. Another, Abigail, married John Sergeant, and
they became the great-grandparents of Mark Hopkins.

† Pronounced "Wah-wam-peck-wah-naunt," no accent.

"They're a fine Scottish couple pioneering in the forests. But they scarcely speak English. They're from the He-lands."

As the evening grew late, Sergeant said: "I am glad you are giving your life to Indian missions. I've been sick and tired to observe the pains the Romish Church takes in missions, and how careless we are. This excites me to emulation, and should everyone else who professes Christianity in greater purity." They conversed about Jesus; prayed. "It was a sweet evening," wrote Brainerd in his diary.

* * *

Early the next morning, April 1, 1743, the Sergeants waved cheerily to Brainerd as he rode into the forests, bound for Kaunaumeek.

* * *

"Kaunaumeek! twenty miles of riding somewhere in the wilderness between Albany, New York, and Stockbridge, Massachusetts." This was too indefinite, so in the summer of 1947, we traveled Highway 20 between Pittsfield and Albany. About twenty miles west of Pittsfield, there is a whistle stop on the Boston and Albany Railroad, "Brainard Station."

But on that August evening the highway was under repair, the forests were dripping with cold summer rain, motel signs read "No Vacancy," so we went back to Pittsfield. . . . But we came again to Brainard Station in early October, the following year, and still again in late October. There Brainard Station nestled attractively in its Berkshire mountain valley, the Taconics standing up to the north. It seemed certain that this was the very site of Kaunaumeek! The panorama looked charming in Autumn sunshine and Fall tints; but Brainerd esteemed it "the most lonesome wilderness." You must remember, however, that

David was all alone; "no one near who spoke English." Further, he never records himself as one who was disposed to sigh, "Ah! wilderness!"

                              *   *   *

On the night of April 1, Brainerd rode out of the forests into the rough clearing at Kaunaumeek. . . . The light leaking from around the clapboard door of a wilderness shack proved to be the McGinlay home. . . . Here he was to be "entertained"! None can understand the abuse heaped upon that good word until he becomes an itinerant minister!—flocks of noisy children, who regard the weary missionary as a heaven-sent provision for a Roman holiday! unheated rooms. . . .

Brainerd wrote his brother John a month later:

The McGinlay cabin is a half mile from the Indian village where I will work. It is a log room without any floor. . . . My bed is a platform of boards six inches above the ground . . . my meals mostly hasty pudding [half-cooked oatmeal mush], hominy [corn dehusked by violent wood-ash lye], and corn bread baked in the ashes of the fireplace . . . sometimes a little meat and butter.

The stiff journey from New York exacted its usual toll. From April second to sixth, Brainerd was frightfully depressed.

"Waves and billows rolled over my soul. God's mercy seemed clean gone forever."

Nevertheless, despite his weariness, he began his work by walking the distance between McGinlay's cabin and the Indian village. He would have ridden, but there were as yet no corrals for his mare.

He immediately began to instruct the Indians in the faith.

They were kindly and attentive, but without a good interpreter the work seemed impossible. He seemed so unequal to his task, he longed for death exceedingly.

Then he remembered Sergeant's words about the necessity of an interpreter. He returned from Stockbridge, May 2, with John Wauwaumpequunaunt. This young man was an ingenious Indian; a warm-hearted Christian; Massachusetts born; well educated. After a time Brainerd and John moved into the Indian village, and lived together for several weeks in a wigwam. Brainerd launched the arduous construction of a hut for himself, into which he moved July 31.

John spoke both Indian and English fluently. This was a comfort to Brainerd:

"There was now at least one person in this lonesome wilderness with whom he could converse."

John was also an excellent teacher. Why couldn't an Indian school be launched at once with John at the head? Brainerd decided to make a special trip to New York to seek the approval of the SSPCK; and he would return to Kaunaumeek by way of New Haven. He would make another appeal to Yale for reinstatement. The whole affair was so distressing to him, it was hurting his work: "he dared not look the Indians in the face. . . ." Yale coldly rebuffed him.

His anguish was so great as he rode back to Kaunaumeek that a desperate illness overwhelmed him en route.

His soul was in a piteous condition . . . could not hold up his face . . . very hard fever; hard pain in his teeth; pains over his whole body. It was good to get to the Bellamy home in Bethlehem. There he tossed deliriously for almost a week. He thanked God for the Bellamys. They loved him.

Before he was really fit to travel, he set out again for Kaunaumeek. His sense of direction failed him. He became lost in the woods. As he rode, he wished he could drop down in the brakes as one of them and pass into oblivion. That night he was obliged to sleep in the open with a cold drizzle falling.

When the stricken boy despondently rode into Kaunaumeek, his heart was again moved—touched by the affection of "the poor Indians." They stood below his saddle and patted the horse: "they appeared very glad by reason of his return." They too, as well as the Bellamys, really loved him! He fell on his knees and blessed God.

Within a month—in July—he made another trip to Yale, and received the same curt rebuff. In late August, a matter of financing for the new Indian school made necessary still another trip to New York. Once again he would take advantage of his journey: he would attend the September commencement at Yale, and make a final appeal. If he failed this time, the case was closed forever.

September 13. "Rode into New Haven dejected."

September 14. "This day I ought to have taken my degree . . . though greatly afraid of being overwhelmed when I should see my classmates take theirs, yet God enabled me." (Edwards tearfully wrote, "His trial was greater because he would have been valedictorian.")

On the night of September 14 he wrote a letter to Rector Clap, needless in self-abasement. . . .

"He was a sinner against God for saying what he did concerning Mr. Whittelsey, though what he said was only spoken in private. He was also heartily willing to humbly apologize to Mr. Whittelsey, and on his knees ask for forgiveness. . . ."

*   *   *

At this point, we may frankly summarize the entire affair, so far as Yale University is concerned. In the two hundred years that have elapsed since Brainerd's expulsion, many have regretted Yale's failure to make public amends. But, let us in 1949, be fair in our judgment of the University. Redress was undoubtedly

Packet 7

THE DELAWARE RIVER

We recommend that readers in quest of Brainerd make a Delaware River trip. If you desire to do your sightseeing the easy way, you may go, summer or winter, by train. Take the Erie Railroad bus from Rockefeller Center. Board the diesel-powered Erie Limited at Jersey City. After eighty miles you come to Port Jervis and the Delaware River. Those lofty mountains which tumble their forested flanks right down to the river's edge are being taken up in this good year, 1950, by New Yorkers who have made money, and who now are as anxious to get out of New York as formerly they were to get into it. . . . After one hundred and seven miles the train reaches Shohola; after one hundred and twenty-two miles, Narrowsburg; after one hundred and sixty miles, Hancock; after two hundred and fifteen miles, Binghamton. . . .

When you return to New York, take the Delaware, Lackawanna and Western. After one hundred and fourteen miles, you come to the Delaware Water Gap. Ah, Flock of the Pages, we hope the foregoing gives you wanderlust, for which malady no better cure can be prescribed than the journey suggested above. All the while you ride, keep thinking, "This is Brainerd Country." And to make it complete, go into the train diner and order some Indian Pudding. Brainerd did not care for it as a steady diet. Possibly you may not. But what a dish of local color!

DELAWARE RIVER NEAR MONGAUP, N. Y.

"At Mongaup he saw for the first time the Delaware River, far below, shimmering like a ribbon of silver in the May sun."

Photo, courtesy the Erie Railroad

THE DELAWARE WATER GAP

"He remembered the words of the old trapper . . . forty miles downstream the waters cut through the Kittating Mountains, forming a great water gap."

Photo, courtesy the Lackawanna Railroad.

Photo of a painting, courtesy of the Northampton County Historical and Genealogical Society

EASTON, AS SEEN FROM PHILLIPSBURG

Painted about 1810. Artist unknown.

"His destination was not far beyond. Sixty miles down stream lay the Indian village of S a k h a u w o t u n g, wedged into the forks of the Delaware."

appropriate while Brainerd lived; appropriate even in the time of Brainerd's contemporaries who survived him. But at this late date, any attempt *officially* to reverse the tragic action of two centuries ago would be clumsy indeed.

There is a curious *lex non scripta* for shriving institutions. The *monetary* obligations, if an institution is to be absolved, must be paid or rightfully cancelled. But as to the *moral* obligations— these can never be settled by resolutions! After time has passed, honor is regained for institutions solely upon the evidence of change in the heart of the constituency. There is a magnificent passage in a certain Old Book which portrays the restoration of a people guilty of the crime of the ages. It was not accomplished by a resolution! The record sublimely narrates, "They shall look upon me whom they have pierced, . . . as one that is in bitterness for his firstborn" (Zech. 12:10).

And to the Yale of today, Brainerd is as a "firstborn." Every phase of my research was accorded not only courtesy, but deep interest by today's Yale, as the chapter "Thank You, Neighbors" will show.

There is a beautiful reminder of David at Yale today. Eight two-story men's dormitories stand just beyond the entrance of the Sterling Divinity Quadrangle at 409 Prospect Place. The second house, beginning at the northeast, is, to quote from page 13, *1946-1947 General Information of the Yale Divinity School,* "to honor David Brainerd." The inscription upon the building is amazing:

"David Brainerd, Class of 1743."

Yale University officially affirms "David Brainerd is an alumnus of this School"! We will let them work the proof out for themselves, and give them every help we know in the task. That's

H

the way the Yale of '49 wants it! And that's the way we want
it! And if the saints in glory are at all interested in our mortal
values, that's the way David Brainerd wants it! One of today's
leaders in Yale writes:

> "It would seem that the University has confessed her
> errors, and paid tribute to the greatness of the man's total
> career."

*   *   *

Any further detail upon the Yale affair is but a burden to the
pages. We will just leave it; though all who read will be aware
of the sinister pall it cast over Brainerd until the angels told him
it really did not matter. . . . There was, however, one bright
spot in the 1743 commencement. He was invited to meet Jonathan Edwards at a reception. And—he met Jerusha Edwards, too!

*   *   *

The annals of the Kaunaumeek Boot School may be quickly
summarized:

During that year he learned how to forage the forests for
a winter's supply of horse food; how to put up hay and fodder;
how to track his horse when it wandered away among the trees.
He mastered the fine art of working under a starvation diet;
how to subsist on Indian entremets; but it cannot honestly be
said he ever learned to like them. He learned how to keep going
though obliged to sleep on straw beds. He mastered all-weather
roughing it as he repeatedly rode to language school. And within
a year, he mastered the Indian language to such a point that,
though he could not preach in it, he could engage in wigwam
palaver.

He also gained that certain touch which comes to a man through building a hut of his own. This achievement greatly diminished wilderness terror. "Blessed be God!" he wrote when the cabin was completed. "He has now given me a place of retirement!"

He further perfected his priesthood in woodland prayer-vigils:

When at times the Indians appeared so senseless that nothing could be done with any effect, and there seemed little of success to comfort him, though he had spent his time in utmost diligence, he retired to his Berkshire Solitary Place. There he fasted and prayed. There he found, as have many before and since: Fasting and prayer are the only weapons made to prosper against the Satanic blackness of paganism.

*   *   *

A year of labor at Kaunaumeek concluded the time originally suggested by the SSPCK. Brainerd saw that the limitations there were too great. His work was finished. There were only a few Indians. The Whites were bent upon stealing their land. He urged the Indians to move down to Stockbridge where Mr. Sergeant would look after them. Sunday, March 11, he preached his last sermons.

The next two days he spent in briefing the Red Men for their migration, then he immediately headed for New York to report to the SSPCK. The Commissioners heard his report. They seemed delighted. Mr. Pemberton, speaking for the group, said:

"Now Mr. Brainerd, return to Kaunaumeek, pack up, and proceed immediately to the Forks of the Delaware."

*   *   *

At last he was headed toward the field upon which his heart was set! He remembered what the old trapper in Bethlehem had told him: "No need to go down to New Jersey: cut right across the wilderness to Port Jervis, and thence down the Delaware."

April 30 he returned to Kaunaumeek,

so ill he did not enjoy his own house. . . . Early morning May 1, he mounted his mare and set forth for the Forks of the Delaware, so disordered that little or nothing but blood came from him.

Small wonder! In the six weeks required for closing the Kaunaumeek work, he had ridden over four hundred miles, cared for endless detail, preached frequently en route to New York and return!

But he had chosen to go! And now no power but death could stop him!

XII

The Forks of the Delaware
(MAY 12, 1744—MARCH 20, 1747)

*This chapter brings us to Easton, Pennsylvania,
where highways, canals, and railroads make such a
spill and pelt about the confluence of the Delaware
and Lehigh Rivers. So far as our tale is concerned,
these modern impertinences will have to be dis-
solved. . . .*

*As the industrial confusion melts away, an ancient
Indian village, Sakhauwotung, reappears in the Forks
of the Delaware. Forests primeval replace rolling
and flour mills, lock, wire, and cordage factories.
Suddenly our eyes rest upon a young man who makes
a romance of laying down his life for marginal peoples.*

A biography of the Delaware River, since that literary conceit has become so popular, could well be titled *The Colonial Low Level Route Through the Alleghanies.* . . . Brainerd's eyes lingered on the tali of Mount Minnsi and Mount Tammany, as he moved southward that first time, riding down the Delaware River, through the Water Gap. That was a great while before chambers of commerce began to exploit the wonders of the River.

(Sketch Book)

AY 8, BRAINERD REACHED FISHKILL, just east of modern Beacon, in the Province of New York. The wilderness suddenly assumed a savage aspect; "civilization was falling behind." He began to pray constantly during the long saddle-hours:

Dear Lord, my heart is ready to sink with the thoughts of my work . . . alone in the wilderness! But it comforts me to think of Abraham going out not knowing whither. I beseech Thee, go with me to the Forks of the Delaware.

Acting upon the advice of the old trapper at Bethlehem, he turned southward along the east bank of the Hudson River. . . . Just north of Bear Mountain, he swam his horse to the west bank on the faintly marked trail that ran through the rough forests toward Port Jervis, forty miles away. Somewhere between Peekskill and Port Jervis he came upon a large Indian camp. Here was an opportunity to preach Christ.

"He greeted them in a friendly way, then discoursed concerning Christianity. They received him kindly, but displayed little interest in his message."

Thursday, May 11, he reached Mongaup on the Delaware. He rode out upon a clearing at the north rim of the valley, and paused a moment to regard the magnificent view. He saw, far below, for the first time, the Delaware River shimmering like a ribbon of silver in the May sun. An emerald green island lay midstream. The sight brought to his mind the words of the old trapper,

"Forty miles downstream from the place where the trail meets the river, the stream cuts through the Kittating Mountains, forming a water gap. Sixty miles downstream, there is an Indian village, Sakhauwotung."

Saturday night, May 13, the weary traveler reached the Indian village, Sakhauwotung,* wedged into the Forks of the Delaware.

No "far away place" connected with Brainerd's labors proved so difficult to locate as the Forks of the Delaware. The research brought out several candidates; one, a point near Hancock, New York. There the East and West Branches of the Delaware, tumbling down from the Catskills, unite. Was this "the Forks"? This is an area of great beauty and natural charm. But, of necessity, it had to be ruled out. Every account of Brainerd's Delaware Mission affirmed "the Forks" were "near the present site of Easton, Pennsylvania."

But there are no Forks of the Delaware near Easton! There are indeed at Easton notable river forks where the Lehigh and Delaware Rivers unite. This simply had to be the location of Sakhauwotung. Perhaps the junction was anciently called "the Forks," and later folks added, incorrectly, the phrase "of the Delaware." But this explanation limped wretchedly. Further investigation was necessary.

It was a great day in the Broad Brim Studio when Gilbert S. McClintock's magnificent book, *Valley Views of Northeastern Pennsylvania*† arrived. Front and back of his book, Mr. Mc-Clintock reproduced an ancient map as board-back and flyleaf illustrations. In the corner of this map is this legend:

---

* Pronounced "Sak-haw-wo-tung," no accent.
† Published 1948, by the Wyoming Historical and Geological Society, Wilkes-Barre, Pennsylvania.

A Map of
Pennsylvania
Exhibiting
Not only the Improved Parts of that Province but also
Its Extensive Frontiers
Laid down from actual surveys
And chiefly from the late map of W. Scull
Published in 1700
And Humbly Inscribed
To the Honorable
Thomas Penn and Richard Penn, Esquires
True and Absolute Proprietaries and Governors of the
Province of Pennsylvania
and the territories thereunto belonging

*   *   *

Upon looking at the reproduction of this ancient map, my eye was instantly caught by the Lehigh River, as it circles about Bethlehem, then runs in a northeasterly direction until it empties into the Delaware at Easton. But—*on that old map,* the Lehigh bore the name, *"West Branch of the Delaware River"!* Everything harmonized! Easton *was* on the Forks of the Delaware! and Easton was just where Sakhauwotung once stood! At one time the Lehigh River was called "the West Branch of the Delaware"!

*   *   *

When Brainerd arose from his bed of straw Sunday morning, he was fatigued and depressed by the one hundred and twenty mile ride, laboring through rains and hardships. . . . Indian children shouted at play among the wigwams . . . there appeared to be no Sabbath . . . but in the evening after preaching to the Indians, his heart began to be encouraged. . . . Here he was, at last, on the Forks of the Delaware River!

The Delaware River! How could a full-length portrait of
Brainerd be painted without that stream in the background? Ah,
good readers, you can no more separate Brainerd from that river
than you can properly think of Dan Crawford apart from Africa's
Tall Grass Country. Therefore, we feel obliged to present—
though with sparing words—the Delaware River System.*

                         *   *   *

Let us assume a position on the skyline of the Catskills . . .
and let us also assume that as yet no pioneers have come to this
wilderness.

Look northward: those waving lines below are such streams
as the Schoharie, marking their courses through the forests to the
Mohawk River; the Mohawk in turn to the Hudson, and the
Hudson to the Atlantic. Over in those vast woodlands shall someday stand the City of Electricity, the City of Presidential Lobbies,
and the Bejewelled Dame of Manhattan Island.

Look southward. The rough shoulders which the Catskills
thrust into the clouds continually shake out the showers, and
a company of wild mountain brooks are born. These streams
go rowdying down to form the Delaware River—

"Wild flowing torrents, turbulent mountain streams, twisting about the
bases of high precipices, rivers which never knew a master, rush treacher-
ously from rock to waterfall." (Wildes)

A specimen of these torrents is the Beaverkill, whose cold
trout waters would delight any Izaak Walton. . . . In the
Catskill foothills you see a magnificent band of cathedral-like
pines, and, interspersed, open vales. Someday, shortly before

---

* A book by Harry Emerson Wildes, *The Delaware*, is commended to readers who desire
greater detail. Its piquant pages could have been written only by an author whose shadow
fell often on its waters—as did ours!

the Revolution, a race of hardy whites, living on sowbelly and beans, such chaps as Dan Skinner, will widen those open vales into farms. They will fell the pines, cut them into eighty-foot lengths, raft them down to Philadelphia. There, these "fine sticks" will be cut by British shipbuilders into masts for brigs and sloops and snows.* After selling this lumber, the timbermen will walk back to the Catskills, four hundred miles, their pockets jingling with gold.

Look westward. Two large streams are formed of the mountain torrents, running about sixty miles apart in a westerly direction. . . . But which is the Delaware River? Who knows? To this day men quarrel as to the true source of the Delaware. One farmer "up there" is reported to have affirmed that the source was "the east eaves of his house!" Early settlers neatly avoided the problem by calling these twin streams the "East Branch of the Delaware" and the "West Branch of the Delaware."

After the East and West Branches unite where someday Hancock, New York, will stand, the resultant river outgrows its mountain adolescence, and begins a course, like a stately dowager, to the Atlantic Ocean. Let us follow the enlarged stream; but remember, we are still thinking in terms pre-Colonial. Many years later this river will be given a commission as a boundary line for states, separating Pennsylvania from New Jersey; then New Jersey from Delaware, before the waters are finally poured into Delaware Bay.

From Hancock the river flows easterly towards Port Jervis, and there, evidently unhappy about the mountains which wall it from the Atlantic, it makes a thrust as if to break through. Being flung southwesterly, it flows along the Poconos, where if

* A "snow" is a square rigged vessel, now rare, differing from a brig only in having a trysail mast close abaft the main mast.

you ride in September, as we did, you will pass through a magic canopy of parti-colored oaks and maples flaming with autumn. The rhododendrons are behind, but laurel and gray-green buckwheat appear.

Near Stroudsburg, Pennsylvania, the Delaware, again becoming impatient with the mountains hedging it from the Atlantic, again makes an attempt to break through—and this time succeeds! It charges straight at the Kittatings, a spur of the Blue Ridge Mountains, apparently severs a sizable peak and makes two of it— Mount Tammany on the New Jersey side, 1600 feet; and Mount Minnsi, on the Pennsylvania side, 1500 feet. The resultant two-mile canyon is one of the few places in North America where a continental divide is split asunder. A few miles south and west, the Lehigh River duplicates the feat.* These cleavages are now called "The Delaware Water Gap" and "The Lehigh Water Gap."

But you are to remember, as we resume our primeval pilgrimage down the Delaware, that its waters are like James Whitcomb Riley's Deer Creek,

> "Flowin' by you
> Jess as clear as clear kin be."

Overhead there is no smog from an unrestrained industrialism; no burden of acid wastes, deadly bacteria, or human excreta in the stream.†

---

* How was this done? "Ancient rivers once flowed *north*, at right angles to Kittating fault lines," affirm the ingenious geologists. "They nibbled through. Later—oh, much later— the young Delaware and Lehigh Rivers borrowed the ancient beds and flowed *south*. . . ." While we're at it, let us get our mountains straight. The Kittatings are spurs of the Blue Ridge Mountains; the Blue Ridge, a chain of the Alleghanies; while the Alleghanies are a segment of the giant mountain system, the Appalachians, running from the Gulf of St. Lawrence to middle Alabama.

† An example of how eastern American rivers have been abased since Brainerd's day may be found in Colliers, October 16, 1948, "Our Poisoned Waters": "The navy refused to bring its ships into the Delaware River . . . the smell is unbearable . . . the water corrodes the ships' sides."

Let's proceed a little farther down the Delaware as it ran two hundred years ago. Those fine open spaces will someday be widened into farms: here American cities will stand—Trenton, Camden, Wilmington. You see Indians fishing for fine fat shad with nets made of fox-grape vines; you hear the splash of otters, see flocks of wild turkeys. . . . There near Trenton we see the mouth of a little creek, almost hidden by trees. Six miles up the creek is the Indian village, Crossweeksung. *Will you remember that?* We shall have more to tell you about Crossweeksung in the chapters that follow.

And, finally, we reach Delaware Bay and the Indian River oyster beds; northward in the gray mist is the sandy tongue of Cape May; and in the distance, the Atlantic Ocean. . . . If any should object to the length of these paragraphs, we must say, it's just about time somebody did this work! Brainerd should no longer be suffered to remain a geographical orphan!

* * *

But alas! there were gobblety gooks in America two hundred years ago! Brainerd had scarcely reached the Delaware River before the SSPCK ordered him back to Newark. They wished to ordain him! This time, he cut across the New Jersey coastal plains. The weather was "June-hot, muggy and sticky." Upon arrival at Newark, he was ill several days.

The Presbyterians proceeded with his ordination, beginning June 11. The text assigned him for his extempore sermon, June 12, was Acts 26:17-18: "Delivering thee from the Gentiles!" Very appropriate, we should say. . . .

Brainerd intended to start back to the Forks June 13, but as a result of the double forest journey, his head pain returned, and he tossed deliriously for six days in the home of a friend at Elizabethtown. When, June 19, he was again able to start for the Delaware, he could scarcely mount the saddle, he was so weak.

But the clumsy planning of the SSPCK was as nothing compared to the hardships and trials ahead of him at Sakhauwotung.

XIII

Powwows and Poopoohs

(THE FORKS OF THE DELAWARE, *Cont'd*)

*In which we note that the sagamores of paganism are remark-
ably versatile fellows. They are at home on either side of the
battle. On the Red side they appear as superactive powwows,
clad with a maximum of paint and feathers, yelling like banshees
as they treat indigestion or bless a hunting trip. . . . On the
White side, they appear as plausible poopoohs, garbed with a holiness like that of Uriah Heap, mouthing sweet corn as they
disparage evangelical labors or justify "white advance." But both
are brothers under the skin, and both are the sworn enemies of
men like Brainerd.*

"To the eye of reason, everything that respects the conversion of the poor heathen is as dark as midnight." (Memoirs)

Packet 8

CROSSWEEKSUNG

Nineteen miles northward from Philadelphia lies Crossweeksung-in-the-woods. The name means "Divided Creek." It is a village whose streets were determined by ancient Indian trails. Once bark canoes darted up and down the stream, to and from the Delaware River, six miles away. But today, "it's just a place on the *old* road between Philadelphia and New York."

VILLAGE STREET SCENE
Crosswicks (Crossweeksung), New Jersey

•

THE QUAKER HOUSE
Crosswicks (Crossweeksung), New Jersey

NOW BRAINERD'S LABORS AT THE Forks of the Delaware were promptly opposed by a pair of inimical forces—he knew not which was the stronger. In the background stood savage hatred engendered of white villainy and objectified by Indian powwows, uttering excited incantations and shaking devilish rattles. "Christian no good," they said. "Him drink, lie, steal, go to jail more than Indian."

In the foreground stood the forces of so-called civilization, animated by the "lofty" ideal: "Get while gettin's good," and objectified by white poopoohs, muttering pious twaddle about "native religions" and acting like the devil himself. "Let the poor Indian alone," they said. "His belief is the best kind for him. He will only deteriorate under Christianity."

These forces clashed and fought in complicated patterns. The Indians were at war among themselves, and Brainerd's arrival at the Forks of the Delaware was at the most critical time. The Red Boy gangsters of the Six Nations, such men as Corn Planter and Farmer's Brother, were violently assaulting the Mohawks. The White Boy carpetbaggers, land hungry, took advantage of the unrest, and appropriated the ancient lands of the Mohawks. But they did it under a guise of "Christian motivation."

"Such Christians," Brainerd wrote, "have no concern for Christ's kingdom, but had rather (as their conduct plainly discovers) that the Indians should remain heathen, that they may with more ease cheat and enrich themselves by them. . . . They [the white men] are more pressing to me than lack of proper food."

I

All these warring factors regarded Brainerd as a common enemy.

As a result he felt as lonesome as if he were banished from all mankind. . . . He knew not where to go. . . . Everything conspired to make his affairs dark and gloomy. But he saw through the antagonism which both sides vented upon him and his purposes—*their hope of gain was gone.*

* * *

The analyst who wishes to enlarge upon the importance of Brainerd's labors at the Forks of the Delaware by citing his evangelical triumphs will search in vain. His work at the Forks, outwardly, was a failure. It does deserve a high place in Brainerd's life; but not as an account of a great awakening, such as occurred at Crossweeksung; neither by reason of a master achievement in secular training, as at Cranberry.* If we had no other criteria for judging Brainerd than his outward success at Sakhauwotung, his life was mediocre.

But the interval at the Forks of the Delaware deserves high valuation in Brainerd's career, for thereby he himself was thoroughly equipped. Here he was forced into the trenches, and "learned to fight the wiles of the Devil." Kaunaumeek was a boot school for *practical living:* Sakhauwotung, a combat zone for *practical fighting.* And anyone who knows military affairs is keenly aware that a man may *train* for a decade without becoming a veteran. It takes a skirmish, so it has been said, to make a man battle-wise.

The Delaware River days did not greatly affect the war score; but they did produce a warrior. And what historian wishes to demean Bull Run when he finds it is part of the price of Appo-

---

* Throughout this book we will retain the ancient names of the New Jersey villages, rather than the modern forms "Crosswicks" and "Cranbury."

mattox? The *incidence* of the Forks, therefore, is of minor importance: we shall have eyes chiefly to the *co-incidence.*

* * *

"It seems impossible ever to go through with this mission," Brainerd wrote. "But, I entertain no notion of quitting my business among the poor Indians."

Dark as it was, he reasoned, there must be a way. So he redoubled his interest in the Hand Book of Tactics which makes men wise unto salvation. In the shack beside the River, which he purchased and remodeled, he spent every available hour in Bible reading. . . .

His faith was much strengthened by observing such things as the wonderful assistance God afforded His servants Nehemiah and Ezra in re-establishing His ancient Church. . . .

One morning in June, 1745, as the fragrance of the woollywaxen forest buds filled the cabin, his attention was remarkably drawn to the ninth chapter of Daniel.

He was impressed by the importunate character of Daniel's prayers as he faced spiritual crises. He noted a certain curious quality in Daniel's prayers—repeated confession of *his own* sin and guilt; repetition of deep sorrow over his own confusion of face. Then, the prayers bemoaned the general lack of intercession among believers, in an evil day. He ended with a passionate cry that God's fury be turned from Jerusalem.

This was the invariable prayer agenda Daniel observed. Then— Brainerd found a sentence in the ninth chapter which roused him like a silver bugle. It was the kind of text a dominie finds, feeds upon for himself, then can scarcely wait for the Sunday service—

"YEA, WHILES I WAS SPEAKING IN PRAYER, EVEN THE MAN
GABRIEL, WHOM I HAD SEEN IN THE VISION AT THE BEGIN-
NING, BEING CAUSED TO FLY SWIFTLY, TOUCHED ME ABOUT
THE TIME OF THE EVENING OBLATION. AND HE INFORMED
ME, AND TALKED WITH ME, AND SAID, O DANIEL, I AM NOW
COME FORTH TO GIVE THEE SKILL AND UNDERSTANDING."
—*Daniel 9:21-22.*

Brainerd's eyes filled with tears. It was just as if he had seen
Daniel transformed before his eyes, changed from an unimportant
servant to a conquering gladiator. . . . Brainerd perceived immediately that:

Whenever God designed to bestow any great mercy on the church,
He called out His servants in prayer and made them wrestle with Him!
Well, that was what he—David Brainerd—would do—copy Daniel's
pattern of intercession.

                          *   *   *

On almost the day of his arrival at Sakhauwotung, he had
selected a Secret Place for his Delaware prayer vigils—just as he
had done at Haddam, at Yale, at Kaunaumeek. So, he greatly
increased his prayer time in his forest glade that straddled a wild
ravine. He often tarried whole nights.

"Someone is going to kill him," the poopoohs said. But they
were immediately aware that the eyes of honest frontiersmen were
upon them. The powwows ground their tomahawks. And the
Indians said to them significantly, "This white man different."
So Brainerd continued his vigils, the angels standing guard.
Honest Red and White Men had no desire to kill him. Powwows
and poopoohs didn't dare.

The record of Brainerd's prayer life is offensive to the cold
of heart. He prayed until his knees trembled when he arose. His
fingers, clenched until blood drained from them, would no longer

flex. He besought God for holiness—not for his personal enjoyment, but as a means of able ministering. He rededicated himself repeatedly as he rode the three miles to the wigwams, or back to his cabin. He continued to pray even when he talked with the Indians.

Alone in his cabin, he interceded until he fell asleep on his knees; and then continued in prayer sweetness* while he slept. When the noise of prowling forest animals or winter-snapping of forest branches awoke him,

the first thing he thought of was this great work of pleading for God against Satan. Over and over he confessed himself so blessed by the glory of this kind of prayer, he had such a sense of divine things, that he was afraid of every thought and every emotion which should draw his heart away from God.

* * *

By-productially, his hours with the Bible produced a notable effect upon his preaching. A rich diversity appeared in his sermons. Sometimes he spent a few moments of introduction in trying to remove Indian prejudices. But he ended up with Jesus.

Sometimes he spoke of home management, and how men should treat their wives. But he ended up with Jesus. "Him talk only about Jesus," said a stolid-faced brave. The same reactions were evident as he preached up and down the river for white settlements. "This man never omits exalting Christ."

* * *

He soon began to realize that his evangelical messages would have to be supplemented. There were certain objective tactics he must employ in the battle against darkness. So he rode miles to

---

* Much of the cloying dulcitude of the language in this book must not be credited to the author. But he wishes to defend it, if it originates with *Brainerd*.

secure lands where his poor Indians could live in peace, and from which "lively whites" dared not drive them. He rode hundreds of miles in special trips to the coastal cities, raising funds, meeting with missionary boards. Rode hundreds of miles into the wilderness ministering to the sick and the dying.

He rode additional miles to defeat the wiles of the firewater devils who sold liquor on credit, then liquidated Indian lands in payment.* "But he raised the small sum of money necessary to free his poor Indians from debt."

At this point we feel obliged to borrow phraseology from the exponents of Social Action. We must record that Brainerd surrendered to the social aspects of the gospel. Of which much more is to be said in Chapter XVI, "Prophet in Overalls." But it should be recorded, before we get to that chapter, that Brainerd never *majored* on the Social Gospel.

*   *   *

The Delaware mission apparently settled down into a drawn battle between Brainerd on one side and the sachems (both kinds) on the other. Had you asked Brainerd he would have said, "I'm losing."

Some degree† of light appeared, it was true. Once the Indians announced a forest frolic, "no bolts barred." He prayed all night that God would stop them: prayed until, when dawn came, his legs sagged as he arose to his feet. But when he reached the woodland that Sabbath morning, they were at it, hell-bent for Sunday.

He had failed. He was so dejected he did not notice they

* The total horseback mileage of his Delaware days, less than two years, runs a staggering total of over four thousand.

† Brainerd's understatements exceed those of the *Breakfast Table Autocrat*. When he prayed, "he received *some* sense of God: he gained *some* degree of holiness": and had Gabriel appeared, he would have written, "That had *some* blessing for me."

stopped instantly when he asked them to do so. Indians had never done *that* before!

* * *

He preached continuously for the near-by settlements where the Irish and Dutch were playing Nature Boys. It's just about time to discount cinema glamour for these frontiersmen, "so pure and simple." Alas, a goodly number of them were neither pure nor simple. They poopoohed Brainerd's moral strictures, and continued getting "high in the forests."

He had failed. He attached no significance to the fact that increasingly as he preached tears appeared in the eyes of the tough whites.

* * *

The Indians appeared to be as wedded as ever to their pagan notions. He could do nothing about it. The fact that when he first began preaching to them only a few came, that increasingly the attendance grew, and that now they were *asking* him "preach more," had no significance. He had failed. "They did not throng home to God."

The powwows had kept the Indians frightened with threats of poisoning and bewitching, if they became Christians. Brainerd decided to challenge their pretenses. One day he paused in a forest sermon and cried, "These medicine men are pretenders. Look!"

He lifted his face and dared the medicine men to strike him! to cause him to fall! to fall dead! . . . The Indians had a guttural chuckle over the discomfiture of the charlatans. The powwows, incensed, made big medicine, and jumped at him from behind trees like lions out of a thicket.

He had failed.

He seemed to regard it as having no importance that a few of
the powwows threw away their snake rattles and burned their
stinking boar-skin kimonas.

* * *

Yes, he had failed. It broke his heart to admit it. Not that he
cared for himself, even if it came to dying. Not at all. Long
ago he had settled those points. Whether he lived or died, it was
not unto himself but unto God. In fact, with such a broken body
he would greatly prefer to be absent from the body, present with
his King. What broke his heart was that the King got no great
name to Himself!

As we read the *Memoirs,* we see the angel appear on the rim
of the pit. But our poor Gideon, threshing grain, has no idea
angels are anywhere near. When will Brainerd's eyes be opened?
Will he remain forever blind to the signs of Visitation?

Will he never discern the significance of honored clergymen
riding out to the wilderness just to meet him? just to hear his
sermons to the poor Indians?

Will he attach no importance to the fact that every pulpit in
New Jersey wants him to supply some Sunday, as well as dear
Brother Beaty's Church over at Neshaminy?

* * *

At the service in Neshaminy so many hundreds rode in to
attend meeting that the congregation had to be adjourned "abroad"
(out of doors). The pale faced, pathetically thin young man,
breathing with difficulty, began to preach. Four thousand hung
on his exposition of Isaiah 53:10: "Yet it pleased the Lord to
bruise him."

* * *

Look, David Brainerd, we've all but lost patience with you! Can't you see that "the man Gabriel" has been caused to fly swiftly to *you?* that he has given *you* skill and understanding, just as he did to Daniel?

"Alas, no! I am a failure. After the service, I could scarcely look anyone in the face, because of the imperfections I saw in my preaching."

*   *   *

But David, how about the next day when the multitudes came back and listened to you preach upon Psalm 17:15, "I shall be satisfied, when I awake, with Thy likeness"? Why, David, there was scarcely a dry eye in the throng.

"Well, I did feel *some* warmth myself. But I judged myself to be such a failure that I wanted to get back to the wilderness where I belonged."

*   *   *

Well, David, we can do no more for you. You have reached the place where God is about to reward your flagellant pace with the rewards of His Grace. And—you can't see it!

*   *   *

Some One Else will have to open your eyes.

XIV

Crossweeksung — Cranberry

(JUNE 19, 1745—MARCH 20, 1747)

The Day of Visitation comes, but our Gideon does not seem to realize it. Not that he ever lacked a heart to glorify God; but he esteemed himself so lowly that, like Job, had God spoken to him, he would have thought it impossible. The King must needs, Himself, open Brainerd's eyes, even as we hoped He would.

"What a revelation of God!" the exultant David wrote to Jerusha.

At Kaunaumeek he had labored a year with no great result; another fourteen months at the Forks of the Delaware with no larger encouragement. But here at Crossweeksung, in less than ninety days, "the poor Indians of a sudden refrained from liquor, though it flowed freely as water. They became marked by serious and savory conversation. They began to love the soul-humbling doctrines of grace, and seem never better pleased than when hearing of the sovereignty of God. I never saw a time like it!"

(Memoirs)

ON SEVERAL OCCASIONS, AT SESSION meetings, Brainerd's ministerial friends, in the Synod of Philadelphia, and Presbytery of New Brunswick, New Jersey, suggested to him that he undertake missionary work among Indians farther down the Delaware River. "At Crossweeksung, New Jersey, near Trenton, there are small settlements of Indians who appear much more amenable to the gospel than most." Brainerd's increasing sense of failure at the Forks of the Delaware made this suggestion seem welcome.

His mind had become "so damped" over the work about Sakhauwotung that he determined to visit the New Jersey field. On the nineteenth of June, 1745, he set out from New Brunswick, and arrived at Crossweeksung the same day. The village was situated in the woodland about eight miles southeast of Trenton. And it will help some readers who have *Zeitgefuhl* to be reminded that in about thirty years after Brainerd arrived at Crossweeksung, George Washington will ferry his soldiers over the Delaware by landing ships, rowboats.

* * *

Let us attempt to gain a more lively idea of the Crossweeksung of 1745.. Why not push the civilization of 1949 out of the picture and replace it with a Colonial proscenium? . . . So we leave Philadelphia! one last look at William Penn hulking in bronze atop the City Hall. . . . The City of Brotherly Love always did give us a damp; those herds of roaring chariots, running one way,

141

gutter to gutter, in streets far too narrow! . . . Ah! this is better.
Big Town is shrinking: it has now become 15,000. We go over
the Delaware to Camden-in-the-sticks. . . . Fine stands of timber
and a few open fields are about us.

After twenty-eight miles of timber road, we come to Borden-
town—pardon, Barden's Town! . . . Three miles east, we reach
Crossweeksung. Nineteen miles northward is Cranberry-in-the-
woods, the place where fresh horses are hitched to your sturdy
coach. You think, "I wonder if those are the towns called Crosswicks and Cranbury in 1949?" That's right—but forget it. This
is 1745, not 1949. If it helps any, remember that thirty-three miles
to the east is the same old Freehold; and up there a short distance
is the same old Princeton. It's a beautiful country, this tidewater
farm land! To be sure, there are but few houses here in 1745.
But, such as there are, unlike veterans' houses of 1949, they have
been built to stand for decades, not to fall down prior to the last
installment. That big building up at village center, the Quaker
House, will look very rugged indeed in 1949.

*   *   *

You are amused by the crooked streets of Crossweeksung. They
twist about like the layout of a very modern subdivision. Actually,
however, the Indians will tell you, "White man makum streets
from Indian toe paths." . . . We find the word "Crossweeksung"
means "divided creek," and what a lovely stream it is! Bark canoes
dart up and down, coming from, or going to the Delaware River
six miles away. But that's far better than the Jijoe Juggernauts
that bully small passenger cars on the Philadelphia free-way in
1950!

While we are about this business of restoration, why not bring back a few of the 1745 Colonial neighbors? Likely you thought of them as bogtrotters, of the Chaw-Bacon Tribe. Far from it! Dressed as they are in powdered wigs, they esteem themselves cosmopolites indeed. "The frontiersmen [they will tell you] are o'er yon in the timber—at such places as Harrisburg."

* * *

Step up and meet certain of these old-timers.

Here is the new pastor of the Presbyterian Church at Cranberry—Rev. Charles MacKnight, settled 1744. The Cranberry pulpit committee, when they "supplicated the Presbytery for supplies," made an excellent case for themselves: The town was important; right on the busy post-road from Philadelphia to New York. Near the church was one of the three relay stations (and taverns) where they changed horses (and indulged in horse's necks). The church edifice, very beautiful and new, was erected in 1740. . . .

When young Mr. MacKnight arrived, no one was disappointed. Young he was, and highly educated; dynamic, sympathetic, good looking—just like a thespian Oscarman! Why, bless me, he's good enough for Tenth Church, Philadelphia!

Your 1949 auto map bears a legend: "Presbyterian Church Two Hundred Years Old." You think, "Then Brainerd must have preached there." When you think that, you must take a grain of salt. The edifice of 1949 was not built until about 1790. Cranberrians will retort: "Perhaps so, but the present building has the same plan and is constructed of the same lumber."

Tarry a moment while we present other specimens of Tidewater worthies in 1745. Here is William Tennent, who conducts the Log College at Neshaminy, near Philadelphia. Whitfield says, "Old Mr. Tennent is like an ancient prophet." He is a tall Scotchman who has four equally tall sons—all Ireland born: Charles, William Jr., John, and Gilbert. William Jr. is able to converse in Latin as well as you do in English, which may sufficiently cushion any suspicion of boasting. Fact is, he talked Latin too much, and it killed him!

But at the funeral, the corpse revived. . . . Now he is pastor of the Church at Freehold, and still shows signs of life. Theological students walk twenty miles to look into his long equine face, topped with a blue-white wig, and enjoy his fine radio presence (pardon the anachronism). What a man! a nonpareil kidder, judge of good horses, and a Colonial Chrysostom!

*   *   *

The woods are full of men in this year 1745, calibered like Preacher Tennent and his sons. There are, for example, Jonathan Dickinson, Ebenezer Pemberton, and Aaron Burr. Burr is to marry Esther, one of Jonathan Edwards' daughters. He is supervising a little college now meeting in the front room of his parsonage at Newark. Certain men have been so perturbed at the treatment Yale accorded Brainerd that they've organized the new college. "You mean Princeton?" That's right.

The Crossweeksung-Cranberry communities of 1745 are not so primitive after all. The citizens talk knowingly of burl chopping bowls, new cylinder-and-shaker threshers, Greek particles, and red buttermilk paint. "Well, then, this was after all not exactly wilderness in 1745." That's just what we wanted you to say! When Brainerd considered the beginning of a work there, it was as if a missionary on the Ox Bow Grade contemplated the beginning of a branch in Phoenix, Arizona.

"But," you think, "what about all those wild Indians running around at Crossweeksung?" Nothing at all, my friend: just

Packet 9

SOUND IN THE MULBERRIES

EDIFICE OF THE CHURCH AT CRANBURY, NEW JERSEY
Photo, courtesy First Presbyterian Church

"Since the church at Cranbury is two hundred years old, Brainerd must have preached there," I mused. But romancing had to be deflated. This edifice was not erected until about 1790. "But anyhow," I thought, "it is on the same plan, and built largely of the same lumber."

Brainerd at the Historic Aftermeeting,
Crossweeksung,
New Jersey,
August 9, 1745

*From an old
Aberdeen woodcut*

Brainerd spoke at this aftermeeting on Luke 14:16-23 (Go into the highways . . . compel them to come in). "The power of God seemed to descend like a rushing mighty wind. . . . I stood amazed."

•

The old powwow turned upon Mutto. Mutto shouted, "Do your worst with me! Once I was a conjurer, and perhaps a better one than you! But when I took Jesus my witchcraft left me, And so would yours, if you got the word of God in your heart!"

Furious Powwow Assaulting Mutto, Forks of the Delaware

*From an old
Aberdeen woodcut*

nothing at all. Drive into Phoenix, Arizona's capital, any Saturday night via South Central Avenue, and note the long line of heavy Studebakers (wagons, not autos) bearing Indian families from Sacaton, on a week-end shopping tour. Note the women with bright colored blankets over their shoulders, beaded moccasins on their feet. . . . America has always been very deliberate about the matter of picking the basting threads from her civilization.

* * *

Brainerd found, upon his arrival at Crossweeksung,
the savages in these parts very much scattered, not more than two or three families in a place . . . miles apart. But they were well disposed, not apt to cavil as elsewhere.

He arranged a preaching service. Four women and three children attended! But these four women, like the woman of Samaria, went abroad and told others of the missionary. Attendance increased rapidly— ten, twenty, thirty, then forty.

Brainerd rode over to Cranberry and Freehold to tell Brothers MacKnight and Tennent the good news. He wrote a letter to Jerusha:

"I am not nearly so anxious to die as formerly. I am now willing to live! I begin to think much of a home of my own, and my own fireside."

Attendance continued to increase. Presently the Indians said, "We want two services every day." How could they live so far away and attend two services a day? "We makum big camp for meeting right here." But how will you eat? They answered by walking a short distance into the woods, killing three fat deer, and preparing a venison barbecue.

Brainerd objected to preaching twice a day; he was not well. He could not preach twice a day. "Very good. Then we listen to Fautaury. Him talk good, too." Of all things! they desired

K

to hear Moses Finda Fautaury* whom they had so lately desired to kill!

Something was in the air!

At this point Brainerd felt it necessary to return to the Forks of the Delaware. William Tennent agreed to open his parsonage for such of the Indians as desired to carry on during Brainerd's absence.† Something *was* in the air. Companies of Indians walked the thirty miles and packed out the Freehold parsonage!

Brainerd, upon returning to Crossweeksung, August 1, found that interest had not declined: it had deepened! As a matter of fact, by means of "the jungle radio" the influence of Crossweeksung was sensed even at the Forks. Concern mounted in the New Jersey meetings from August 4-7. "Even the White Heathen began to attend as if for their lives." August 6 there was the first convert: an Indian woman, who cried that she "wanted Jesus to wipe her heart quite clean."

Thursday, the eighth day of August, 1745, seventy-five Indians ringed about Brainerd as he preached. There was a tenseness in the meeting. His text was Luke 14:16-24: "Go out into the highways and hedges, and compel them to come in." Fautaury's face glowed as he interpreted.

Then of a sudden, at the after meeting, a number of natives began to cry, "Guttummauhalummeh!" ‡

Then of a sudden, at the aftermeeting, a number of natives ing mighty wind, and with astonishing energy bore down all before it. . . . It seized the audience almost universally . . . scarcely one was able to withstand the shock . . . old men and women who had been drunken

---

* Pronounced "Faw-chaw-ry," no accent. A full account of this Indian convert is reserved for Chapter XX, "Indian Summer."

† The reader will remember that Brainerd's commission covered the territories of the Delaware and Susquehanna Rivers. He did not abandon the Forks when he opened the New Jersey field.

‡ Pronounced "Gut-tum-mau-hal-um-meh"—"Have mercy on me!"

wretches, little children, powwows and conjurers were brought to cry for mercy with many tears. . . . As one Indian after another received the Light, he would take others by the hand and tell them about the goodness of God.

* * *

The literary requirements for this chapter are satisfied. Any reader desiring greater detail, more of the individual cases in this Romance of the Twice Born, is referred to the *Memoirs.* There at book length will be found many stirring case histories. But it does appear worth while to sketch somewhat the character of Brainerd's preaching during this awakening, which will be done in the next chapter.

Then, too, it is worth while to sketch an epic phase of the Crossweeksung awakening, wherein Brainerd removed his "poor Indians" to a tract of land, all their own, up at Cranberry. Thus was founded a pioneer Indian Reservation, and there the poor Indians were taught to read and write, to sow and reap. This we shall consider in Chapter XVI.

* * *

But no writer has ever had more dramatic material put into his hands for chapter climax than the words Brainerd entered into the *Memoirs.* At last he looked up and recognized Visitation! He tearfully recorded,

"I stood amazed!"

XV

Sound in the Mulberry Trees

(AUGUST 9, 1745—MARCH 20, 1747)

The life of David Brainerd is of value because it reveals by what means the King sets up His visible kingdom, and how He gathers to Himself a people. The account of the awakening in Brainerd's seaboard parish is a valuable microcosm of evangelism, able to make the Church of any age wise in the lost arts of Pentecost.

"Therefore David inquired again of God; and God said unto him, Go not up after them; turn away from them, and come upon them over against the mulberry trees. And it shall be, when thou shalt hear a sound of going in the tops of the mulberry trees, that then thou shalt go out to battle: for God is gone forth before thee to smite. . . ." (I Chronicles 14:14-15)

ᴘERHAPS THE MOST FELICITOUS
way to analyze the Crossweeksung
awakening would be to cast the account of it into the form of
a modern press interview.

* * *

"So, 'you stood amazed,' Mr. Brainerd. We like the sound of that. You
did not say, 'At last *my* labors have succeeded.'"

"How could I? Just as I wrote of my conversion, 'I scarce reflected
that there was such a creature as myself. My soul was captivated with
the perfections of God.'"

* * *

"But, Mr. Brainerd, many would value some idea as to the part *you*
played, even though you judge it of small importance."

"My part was indeed unimportant. My own heart condemned me. The
only work I had been instrumental in doing among the Indians was the
conversion of Fautaury and his family. I felt I was a burden to the
Honorable Society in Scotland, spending money consecrated to religious
purposes only to *civilize* the Indians.

"I decided to give up at the end of 1745. . . . Then, God made bare
His mighty arm. From this, I learned it was good to follow in the path
of duty, though in the midst of discouragements.

"That is why I esteem the fidelities of Colonial Christians—men like
the Tennents, or Mr. Pemberton, or Mr. Burr. For seventy-five years,
they and their fathers before them had lived lives of good report before
the savages. The confidence of Crossweeksung Indians was in some measure restored. That made it somewhat easier for me to preach. Nevertheless, it was the ancient order—Paul planting, Apollos watering, but
God giving the *increase.*"

* * *

"It must have been impressive, Mr. Brainerd, to hear these Indians
cry out, 'O God! we want Jesus to wipe our hearts clean.'"

151

"That was largely why I stood amazed. They were no longer troubled over *bad conduct* such as drinking . . . they wept over their *bad hearts!*"

*   *   *

"What was the character of your preaching, Mr. Brainerd, when the awakening began? We know you would instantly resent that question if we put it, 'What kind of preaching *brought on* the revival?' "

"Well, naturally I spoke on such things as the attributes of God, the helpless and fallen state of man, and the like. But I have oftentimes remarked with admiration that whatever subject I have been treating upon, I have been naturally and easily led to talk about Christ as the very substance of that subject.

"If I treated on the being and glorious perfections of God, I was thence naturally led to discourse of Christ as the only 'way to the Father.' If I attempted to open the deplorable misery of our fallen state, it was natural from thence to show the necessity of Christ to undertake for us, to atone for our sins.

"If I taught the commands of God, and showed our violation of them: this brought me in the most easy and natural way to speak of, and to recommend, the Lord Jesus Christ as the one who 'magnified the law,' which we had broken, and who was 'become the end of it for righteousness to everyone that believes.'

"Thus I was remarkably influenced and assisted to dwell upon the Lord Jesus Christ. . . . It became unavoidable to discourse of Him . . . and this made possible a continued strain of gospel invitation to perishing souls to come, empty and naked, weary and heavy laden, and cast themselves upon Him."

*   *   *

"Wait a moment, Mr. Brainerd. Your words have a mysterious coloring—'I was led,' 'I was aided.' Would you speak to that point?"

"Of course. I continued in my secret duties: I read my Bible—read until my own sufferings were forgotten: read until I would come to some certain passage that opened with glory. I fed upon it for my own soul's good; then when I came to talk to my poor Indians, I pressed the need in which all of us stood of such a Saviour . . . there was thereupon a great appearance of divine power; promoting convictions began, and comforting for the distressed. Thus, you see, *I was led.*"

*   *   *

"But what about moral instruction, Mr. Brainerd? Did you make plain the obligations of Christian behavior?"

"That work was accomplished by what I call *the moral effects of preaching Christ crucified.* It is worthy of remark that when it was desired that my people be brought to a strict compliance with the *rules of morality,* it was a work produced by the *doctrines of grace.* It seemed unnecessary frequently to repeat and inculcate moral duties, or to expose the contrary vices; for the doctrines of grace had the most direct tendency to correct fallen creatures.

"I remember I was once preaching upon the text, 'He was wounded for our transgressions.' A young Indian mother broke into tears. She said she suddenly became mindful that she had been wickedly cross with her children that day.

"When I preached grace, there was no vice unreformed, no external duty neglected. The abusive practice of husbands and wives in putting away each other and taking others in their stead; drunkenness, the darling vice; vicious practices—these were done away, not because they heard these things spoken against, but because they could no longer continue to offend Him who died for them.

"The reformation of external evils came with the new heart! Remember, however, it was not *preaching* that did it. It was *grace.* Sometimes I was so sick I was obliged to remain seated as I preached. No one on earth would credit anything to the testimony of a man as sick as I."

* * *

"Did you 'summon the thunders of Sinai' when you preached, Mr. Brainerd?"

"I spoke not a word of terror. Such preaching had come into disrepute. To prove that I made no attempt to frighten the Indians into belief, I carefully recorded in my diary every text I used and every service. The Indians were far more impressed by the happiness of the godly than the misery of the wicked; more moved upon by the thought of Lazarus in Abraham's bosom than the rich man in torment."

* * *

"Well, Mr. Brainerd, if you put the premium on any one objective in your preaching, what was it?"

"My first aim was to secure the new birth: moral probity does not appear until men are born again. That order cannot be reversed.

"Certain Indians fell under Quaker preaching at Crossweeksung. They were told that if a man would live soberly and follow the dictates of his own conscience, there was no doubt about his salvation. . . . Indians who had listened to such preaching were harder to deal with than those who knew nothing but pagan darkness.

"But when I spoke on such texts as John 3:16, unspoiled savages fell to the ground in anguish, and remained until they found peace. . . . It was after they were born again that they began to pay their debts, and the like."

* * *

"Mr. Brainerd, was this chiefly a movement among women and children, or did so-called 'hard cases' yield?"

"The most abandoned cases yielded. Hardened sinners seemed immediately to put off their savage roughness. Brotherly love appeared among a people that a short time before were worshiping devils.

"Take the case of the Delaware powwow, Mutto—a depraved conjurer, juggler, murderer.

"When I baptized Fautaury in the Delaware, Mutto was so moved upon that he followed me back to Crossweeksung—eighty miles on foot! As he listened to me—as he expressed it—'talk Jesus all the time,' the spirit of conjuring suddenly left him entirely. 'Preacher drove me into sharp corner,' he said; 'heart got very sad.'

"He continued under conviction a day and a half, attended all services; kept asking, 'When you preach again? My heart love hear about Christ for all.'

"One day he got a lively soul-refreshing view of Christ's way of salvation. He became so zealous for God that when I went back to the Delaware, he followed again. Once while I was preaching there, an old powwow threatened to bewitch me. Mutto jumped to his feet, and the powwow turned on him. Mutto shouted, 'Do your worst with me! Once I was a conjurer, and perhaps a better one than you! But when I took Jesus my witchcraft left me. And so would yours, if you got the Word of God in your heart.'

"When he became a Christian, I decided I would never again despair of the conversion of any man or woman living.

"And, speaking of *hard cases,* white people seemed as deeply moved upon as the Indians. Did I feel liberty to do so, I could tell you of depraved whites, or some merely moral, who were so changed that outside their physical appearance, they could not be recognized."

*   *   *

Now there came to the Broad Brim Study, just as this chapter was being polished for the press, one Dwight H. Small, young Presbyterian dominie of San Jose, much after the cut of Brainerd. I arose and looked outside to see if he had a horse: it was only a Dodge. "Don't cheat us on this book," he said, "as you did in *Man of Like Passions*. Give us the whole story."

"But how can I?" I reproved young Mr. Small. "It's one book I'm writing, not two. Read the *Memoirs* for yourself. Read about Christmas at Crossweeksung, 1745. Read the testimony of the newly saved woman who thus described her emotions: 'By, by, my heart be glad desperately!' Read—why should I, a baffled author, making his way between the devil of book editors and the deep blue sea of avid readers, tabloid your pabulum for you?" That's my answer to those who complain that I've omitted too much.

*   *   *

There is no better case study of "God's appearance from Teman" than the story of Crossweeksung. The matured graces of a New Testament church suddenly appeared among the wigwams. From time to time, Indian converts were observed to disappear into the forests.

"Where were you, Neshamin?"

"I go ask God's blessing on White Men in Scotland who send us our white brother."

The Church in the Wild Wood instantly became missionary-minded without benefit of a single study class. They brought gifts for the work of the SSPCK, gifts of astonishing size for an impoverished people. Better still, they sent deputations of Indian converts to other Indian communities to "talk for King Jesus."

*   *   *

The poopoohs sneered, "It won't last."
BUT IT DID LAST!
There came into the hearts of those Indians qualities that were theirs to have and to hold.

"I know forty-seven men of the wilderness [wrote Brainerd in his last sickness] who were saved: they had been drunkards. But, being saved, they lived soberly when whisky flowed as freely as brooks in the forest. Through rich grace, none of them left their profession."

*   *   *

The Poopoohs always appear when the waters are troubled. "It won't last," they chant in King Dodo unison.
But it does last!
Not only did the converts persevere, but they passed the torch down the lines of their posterity. . . . We found men and women on the reservation in Canada's flatland, whose forebears had been devout Christians since no man knows when. . . . Is there not at Cedar-Palms a scented grass basket, given to Deborah by one of the sweetest-faced Indian women one ever saw?

"This like Jesus," she said. "Him odor of a sweet smell."

And there is a hand-wrought hickory cane given me by the men, whose representative said, with a twinkle in his eye:

"For you, when you get to be old man! Now, walk for Jesus long time!"

Forest pagans never joke; they must wait until the Good One's laughter sounds in their hearts. The Oneidas, however, are marked by graceful humor. Where did they get it? We know! Did we not track the pathetic story of Red Men who, driven from the Delaware country, were nevertheless more than conquerors in the Canadian solitude?

*   *   *

But today there seems to be no trace of this work at Crosswicks or Cranbury. What happened?

In late October, 1948, we stood upon the stone bridge over the Divided Stream, pondering this same question. We dreamed of the canoes which once bore Indians singing the songs of Zion. What became of it all?

*   *   *

It is a melancholy story. When John Brainerd succeeded David, he named the community "Bethel," and it basked for a few years in the glamour of David's fame. Then it abruptly came to an end: "John was dismissed by the Correspondents May 7, 1755, and the mission was closed."

As late as 1800, ruins of the buildings still stood—boys' cabins, mission houses, barns, carpenter shop. But in 1949, there is not a trace! not even a foundation scar. No one seems to have the remotest idea as to the exact location of the ancient compound!

*   *   *

What were the causes behind this forest debacle?

The pestilence of 1750, for one thing, which carried off a considerable number of the converts. . . . The Poopoohs for another: title to Indian properties was finally gotten into "Christian" hands, and the Indians were "helped" to move on.

But new lands were acquired at Brunswick, New Jersey, and

John Brainerd again put in charge. "But it failed again, in a few months."

There must have been other causes. . . . Could one of them have been—*John Brainerd?*

*   *   *

John Brainerd's life was always marked by such sanity, prudence, and—dependability! Today, you would find him consistently grouped with the Co-opie-rators. He was such a good man to have on committees! If a one hundred per cent safe man were desired to act as Chaplain at Crown Point—John got the appointment! Do not misunderstand this paragraph, Flock of the Pages! John was a man of honor; and he had his reward.

Was there not for a long time at Deerfield, New Jersey, a little white slab on a little white church which read:

Here
Under this Building
is buried
John Brainerd
A BROTHER OF DAVID
He was one time Pastor
During the Revolutionary War

*   *   *

And—make no mistake about it—John loved David. Though David always seemed a little on the queer side. Too intense! John first noticed this when they were mere boys, studying together on the farm at Haddam. Sometimes David damped John no end. As for instance, that letter wherein David said John did not seem to *get under* his work as he should; and that David was praying God would send life-changing trials upon John. . . .

But in any case John loved David. Flagellants may be somewhat trying to live with, but they are Rosemary when it comes to Remembrance. . . . Had David only *taken care of himself*, he might have lived to a good old age—like John.

* * *

But of course!

In which event there would have been no Sound in the Mulberries to write about! Both John and David would have long since been forgotten!

Packet 10

CONCERNING THE MEMOIRS

Courtesy, the Library of Congress

Memo of a Contribution Made by David Brainerd to the Cranbury Indian School, in David's Own Hand and Bearing His Signature

TRANSCRIPTION OF THE DAVID BRAINERD MEMO
SHOWN ABOVE

I sold my Tea-kettle to Mr. Jo. Woodbridge, and an Iron kettle to Mr. Tim. Woodbridge, both which amounted to something more than 4 pounds, which I ordered them to pay to you for the School. If that succeeds, I hope you will use the Money that way, if not, you are welcome to it your Self.

As to my blankets, I desired Mr. Woodbridge to take the trouble of turning them into Deer-Skins. If he has not done it, I wish he would, and Send the Skins to Mr. Hopkins, or if it might be, to Mr. Bellamy. . . .

I am, Sir, in greatest haste
Your obedient humble Servant

Rev. Mr. John Sergeant

David Brainerd

Page 47
of John Brainerd's
Journal

Reproduced to provide readers with an enlarged idea of the way pre-Colonials kept their diaries.

Page 1 of the David Brainerd Diary for 1732-1740, presented to Yale University by Mr. Winthrop Brainerd.

Comparing this page with the authentic sample of David Brainerd's hand as found on the memo, we feel that this is not a copy, but a page of Brainerd's veritable manuscript.

Exact size of the sheet on which the diary was written was 15½ x 9½ cm.

XVI

Prophet in Overalls

(MARCH 24, 1746—MARCH 20, 1747)

We behold a band of Crossweeksung Indians marching towards Cranberry, March 24, 1746, armed with—grubbing hoes and grass hooks! On arrival, they assault the brushland, and thus begin work upon a community settlement, wherein Brainerd brings to full bearing the things he learned of John Sergeant. And it is amusing to note how excellently these workers compound faith with farming. As they apply themselves, with their sleeves rolled up, they sing Dr. Watts' "common metre version of the CXXVIIth Psalm"!

Social Service has not only assembled a vocabulary, but also supplied the definitions. In these matters, it is very discriminating. Should Mr. Good Samaritan find his neighbor down with the flu, and should he forthwith don his dungarees, seize his hoe, and assault the Johnson grass on his neighbor's canal— well, that is considerate, and all that sort of thing. But—it is *not* Social Action.

Should Mr. Good Samaritan, however, take note that the dairyman is skimming the milk so much that it is no longer palatable to his neighbor's baby; should he thereupon put on his bow tie, gather some leading citizens, go down in a body to influence properly the City Council—that *is* Social Action.

Having no desire to remove landmarks, it seems necessary to provide our own terminology. We need words that include everything, from barn-raising to barn-storming. Let us think of Mr. Good Samaritan as a Knight in Blue Denim—a Prophet in Overalls.

(Sketch Book)

QUITE A BIT TOO LENGTHY WOULD this chapter become, if all of the subject matter in the *Memoirs* concerning Brainerd's girding himself with a towel to wash the disciples' feet were quoted. We leave the superabundance to writers of well-documented biography. We prefer to imitate a certain device found in Deborah's Needlework Magazine. Therein is a pattern-illustration with the following words: "This design goes entirely around the Afghan"; meaning, of course, the worsted chair cover she was knitting. And, believe it! that small pattern provided an excellent idea as to the appearance of the completed four-by-four blanket. Capital! We'll just yarn off a few paragraph squares—and let your imagination finish the chapter.

* * *

Brainerd applied to himself the Levitical law of priestly stewardship. The Jewish priest, being a man without a farm, received his income from the tithing of farmers. But the priest was himself under the requirements of stewardship, just as much as the farmer. He therefore ought to tithe the tithe. This Brainerd did, and a great deal more!

You see how it worked out in the *Memoirs.* On New Year's Day, 1744, he put down a recapitulation of his charities:

"In about fifteen months past, I have given to charitable purposes about one hundred pounds." Edwards, fearful the readers might not appreciate these figures, made a footnote: "Which was to the value of Ł185 in our bills of the old tenor."

163

It now becomes evident how convenient our new terminology is! There is apparently no way of linking up a Christian's personal stewardship with such a formidable term as "Social Action." But the idea of a man reaching into his jeans to help in good works, fits very nicely into the overall concept.

In addition to such contributions, Brainerd had objectives of his own. For example, he used much of his patrimony to enter and support in Yale a Salisbury, Connecticut, boy who was studying for the ministry. This support continued until Brainerd's death. Whenever convenient, he visited the student; often wrote him. The last letter the young man received (summer of 1747) was in effect a bit of propaganda for flagellant living:

> In these days, we are so strangely amused, that we lose our sense of holiness. . . . I am dying, wholly speechless for hours together. I call upon you to make it your business to live to God.

* * *

Elsewhere in this book reference is made to Brainerd's continual vigilance in checkmating the schemes of white scalawags who designed to foreclose Indian lands on whisky debts. Much of this money he himself contributed. Once he financed a woman schoolteacher (near Kent) when he launched a wigwam school. . . .

* * *

Brainerd was constantly aware of the Indian's practice of raising his family on the borderline of starvation:

> They have been bred in idleness and know little of cultivation. . . . I have felt obliged to instruct them . . . also press them to the performance. . . . The care of managing their worldly business and of checkmating white villains, costs me more labor and fatigue than all my other works.

* * *

When the Crossweeksung awakening came, he saw an opportunity for a full-scale application of his service ideals. Charles MacKnight, pastor at Cranberry, often rode down Sunday afternoons to hear Brainerd preach, visiting with him after service. The first time he heard Brainerd speak of an Indian reservation, he was instantly enthusiastic.

"Fine! but, since you cannot get the kind of tract you need here in Crossweeksung, come up to Cranberry. I know of a section that is just what you want. . . . And you can live with me and Mary in the parsonage as long as you wish."

Brainerd, in company with MacKnight, inspected the land. "Just right," he thought. Then, on the approval of Jonathan Dickinson and the SSPCK, he raised "eighty-two pounds, five shillings N. Jersey currency at eight shillings per ounce," and secured title.

March 23, 1746, he conducted a Promised Land service in the Indian Church:

You must now labor with faithfulness and industry, no longer slothful in business as you were in your pagan state. Planting time is at hand. Be laborious, diligent!

March 24, 1746, the Indians began clearing the land. May 17 the emigrants moved in. There was a stirring Trans-Jordan rally, Brother MacKnight preaching, Brother Fautaury interpreting.

* * *

Then began an epic of improvement, which continued with Brainerd leading until his broken health ended his work March 20, 1747. He taught them to build barns and mend fences, to store wheat, to erect cabins and thus move out of the wigwams. A school, a carpenter shop, an infirmary were erected. A nurse and a schoolteacher were secured. It was a gala day when the teacher arrived, January 31, 1746. The school opened with thirty in the day sessions, fifteen in the night. Brainerd himself handed out the primers, several dozen of them. And we have a good idea as to where he got the money to buy them! (See photo of memo in Brainerd's hand.) We have reason to believe he raised that money by selling another teakettle!

Brainerd, having never cared for hasty pudding, set up classes in cooking! . . . There were also classes in the English language.

Ah, how convenient that literary emancipation suggested by Deborah's Needlework Magazine! Reader, by means of the patterns above suggested, you can complete the entire social service fabric yourself!

*   *   *

The administration of the Cranberry Farms became a historic achievement. In late years, a Princeton man wrote, "Brainerd was a mystic, but his program was eminently practical." Princeton University has always held Brainerd in high esteem. There are four receipts among their other relics, wherein Brainerd acknowledges certain monies received from John Sergeant, Treasurer of the College of New Jersey.

On the nineteenth day of September, 1746, Brainerd, very ill, rode into the little colonial town of Princeton, New Jersey. "He spent the evening with some degree of satisfaction in the home of Pastor Stockston." It is a subject of romantic speculation how much greater would have been his delight could he have envisioned the magnificent university, with its campus and edifices! could he have foreseen the new Firestone Library in which his Hebrew Lexicon would someday be one of the choicest treasures!

On the first anniversary of his New Jersey labors, he made an entry in the *Memoirs,* and copied it in a letter to Jerusha. It was in keeping with his consistent habit of self-effacement:

This day makes up a complete year from the time of my first preaching to these Indians in New Jersey. What amazing things has God wrought.

* * *

We have no disposition to take any of the glory from God, but we must say the King had chosen to depend upon a faithful servant. . . . Once when the schoolteacher was very sick, Brainerd nursed him back to health; taught his classes during the interval.

* * *

It is reported that one day an Indian brave, now dressed in farm togs instead of paint and feathers, leaned on his hoe and said of David:

"Him not only *talk* Jesus all the time.
Him *live* Jesus all the time."

XVII

A Flagellant's Journal

(APRIL 20, 1739—SEPTEMBER 25, 1747)

*Herein we examine the annals of a man com-
pletely mastered and moulded by the doctrines of
self-effacement. The entries evidence ruthless self-
surgery. Self-esteem is exposed, sliced away, and
cauterized as if it were carcinomatous. The author of
the* Memoirs *had in mind autotherapy only; but the
reader soon feels that he, himself, is going under the
knife.*

It is hard to be neutral towards the Memoirs.
*Readers adjudge the book either to radiate heavenly
light or to reek with* mania a potu; *they close the
pages either snarling or sobered.*

"I was greatly exercised with inward trials and distresses all day: in the evening my heart was sunk, and I seemed to have no God to go to. . . ."

* * *

"I was amazed that God should stir up hearts to show kindness to such a dead dog as myself . . . I wondered if I should ever preach again. . . ."

* * *

"I long to be as busy for God as the angels."

(Memoirs)

EADERS MAY ARRANGE THEIR autobiographical books into at least five divisions: Memoir, Memoirs, Annal, Journal, and Diary. Should you be required to undertake such a task, we wish you courage; catalogers would not agree with you—they do not even agree with one another! It is only because of the confusion arising from divided opinions that we dare submit some definitions of our own.

A "memoir" is a biographical history written by one who has been the actor in the drama he records. "Memoirs" (plural) are an account consisting of notices and remarks respecting contemporaneous persons and events, in a familiar style, just as they are remembered by the author. See the difference? . . . Neither do we.

A "diary" is a record of daily events or transactions such as have reference to the writer personally. His book is graded a "journal" if it sounds weighty or abstruse. If the author, while writing, has the sly idea of preaching to someone who is looking over his shoulder, the book becomes an "annal." Should you disagree with all the above, write your own definitions, so that we may disagree with you.

The differences are so subtle that an average man is safe in using the terms almost interchangeably. Sometimes we've wondered if the several labels are not applied, like military titles, to connote relative importance. If the account is light and frilly, it's a "diary"; if well written, its subject matter of great importance, it is "memoirs." Thus Pepys had nice discrimination when he labeled his bedroom journal a "diary"; but Greville, in his opus of courtly stinkers, was much deficient in precision when he called his work a "journal."

The foregoing heartily approved Bonar's judgment when he named M'Cheyne's residual documents *Memoirs and Remains.* And Sereno Edwards Dwight was an intellectual chip off the old block—his great-grandfather Jonathan Edwards—when he called David Brainerd's diary, "Memoirs."

But, however light or heavy, these volumes, if dependable, are of highest value. For, to gain an understanding of life and history, no books can surpass autobiography; and the man who dares to write his diary will be both blessed and chastened by his own pages. Perhaps the top-line books here in Cedar-Palms are these three: St. Augustine's *Confessions,* Bunyan's *Grace Abounding,* and standing just between the two, forming a trinity of great literature, *The Memoirs of David Brainerd.*

*   *   *

As early as April 6, 1740, Brainerd wrote that

"He was relieved from his gloom by passages in his diary."

And when he lay dying, and John Brainerd brought him the *Memoirs*—

"he read his old private writings, and rejoiced for what God had done long ago, which without writing had been utterly lost."

Reader, why not start a diary of your own?

*   *   *

Brainerd began the habit of making daily entries in a diary at least as early as the twentieth day of April, 1739. By the time he went to live with Jedediah Mills, March, 1742, he had already filled two little books. Sometimes reference is made to Brainerd's "Journal." That was, both first and second parts, simply extracts from his *Memoirs* during his work at Crossweeksung and Cranberry. The absurd title, *Mirabile Dei Apud Indicos,* was the feverish effusion of a Scotch publisher, looking for a knockout caption. . . . Just how many separate holographic books there were of Brainerd's *Memoirs,* Edwards never confides; but however many there were, they are the only real source material we have on "how Brainerd occupied his time from day to day, and how he felt about it."

Edwards took the precious manuscripts, particularly the two Brainerd was about to destroy, and by the simple device of inserting his own comments every now and then between daily entries, fashioned a book. Edwards' book was in no sense a biography: more accurately it was an edited autobiography. He never claimed it was a biography. He crossed out many entries "for brevity's sake," and published, 1749, his volume under the title, *Account of the Life of the Late David Brainerd.*

Sereno Edwards Dwight, grandson of Edwards' daughter Mary (1734-1807), one time Pastor of Boston's "Brimstone Corner" (Park Street Congregational Church), and President of Hamilton College, produced a second *Life of Brainerd.* He used his great-grandfather's book, the *Account,* as the basis of his book; and published, 1822, what he called *Memoirs of the Late David Brainerd.*

Dwight's book was a signal contribution by reason of the fact that he not only used his great-grandfather's work to the full, but added priceless data of his own. Dwight's book, in our opinion, merits reprint more than Edwards'. There you will find the editor edited—Edwards' comments commented upon.

For instance, he says: "Edwards in his book omits those parts of Brainerd's diary which were published in the Scotch *Journal*." He signallized this omission by inserting a dash, thus—: "his delicate integrity would not allow him to subject his subscribers to the necessity of purchasing the same matter a second time"! But Dwight, like ourselves, never permitted such delicate integrity to cramp his style. Dwight published everything, including letters of Brainerd's which Edwards never saw, and facts of which Edwards was unaware or which he deemed irrelevant to his purposes.

This volume of Dwight's is a literary curio today, and just to think! we found one floating freely on the stalls of a New York secondhand bookstore!

*   *   *

Nothing worthy of note was added to this bibliography until James M. Sherwood, a Presbyterian minister, published in 1885 his *Memoirs of David Brainerd*.

Dr. Sherwood (1813-1890), though forced by poor health to give up college, and pastoral labors, nevertheless reached the age of seventy-seven, and made a notable record in New York City in the field of religious journalism. His name was editorially associated with Century, Scribners, the *Homiletic Review*, and the *Missionary World*. The fact that he was born in Fishkill, N. Y., where Brainerd camped, 1744, en route to the Forks of the Delaware, stirred his imagination and prompted his volume on Brainerd.

His book is a further editing of Edwards' editing. Its value lies in that Sherwood lived sufficiently remote in time to tell "what became of folks"—the folks who are now too remote for 1949.

Nothing worthy of note was added to the three volumes for nearly sixty-five years. In 1949 the Moody Press published *The*

Life and Diary of David Brainerd, edited by Jonathan Edwards, with introduction and comments by Philip Eugene Howard, Jr. This book is part of the Wycliffe Series of Christian Classics, Wilbur Moorehead Smith, general editor. The chief value of this volume is that it again makes accessible to the public not only Brainerd's *Memoirs,* but also the *Journal,* as Sereno Edwards Dwight published it.

Fortunately, in the production of this book, *Flagellant on Horse-back,* the volumes of Edwards, Dwight, Sherwood, and the Moody Press have all been on the shelves of the Broad Brim Studio. And, in addition, the priceless Volume 8, Sparks' *American Biography,* containing the *Life of Edwards* by Samuel Miller, and the *Life of Brainerd* by W. B. O. Peabody; loaned to me by The Library of Congress.

* * *

"But what about the original manuscripts?"

A good idea of their appearance may be had from John Brainerd's *Manuscript Journal,** which is in the Library of Princeton University. John imitated David's technique of Journal making. Look at a page of John Brainerd's book, then look at the specimen of David's hand and signature reproduced in this book and— well, what more do you want?

* * *

"But what about *the original manuscripts?*"

My, but you are persistent! We'll tell you just the way we heard it. There were certain gentleman's agreements when Brain-

---

* A little notebook of sixty pages, covering the period January to October, 1761, bound so tightly it cannot be opened wide enough for photography. There are also among the Princeton treasures six receipts in Brainerd's hand and signature, acknowledging monies received for Indian Mission work from John Sergeant, Treasurer of the College of New Jersey—"Princeton" to you!

erd turned over his booklets to Edwards. Dwight says Brainerd "left all his papers in the hands of that *gentleman* [Edwards], that he might dispose of them as he thought would be most for God's glory, and the interest of religion." Edwards edited, then published them.

"But why did Edwards withhold such priceless documents?"

He did not withhold them. He edited, published, and then *disposed of them!*

* * *

In the Rare Book Section of the Library of Yale University, there is a collection of manuscripts associated with the life of David Brainerd. These may be grouped under two headings:

(1) A copy of Brainerd's *Diary*

(2) A "few detached leaves" from his *Diary*.

* * *

As to the first group, Mr. Henry M. Fuller, Reference Librarian, Yale University Library, writes me:

"It is a manuscript copy in an eighteenth century hand, covering the years 1732-1740. Since it is not signed, one cannot tell whether it was the original kept by Brainerd, or a copy made by some contemporary. It was given to the Divinity School by Mr. Winthrop Brainerd, a graduate of Sheffield Scientific School of Yale University. Winthrop Brainerd is descended from James Brainerd (David's grandfather), the second son of Daniel Brainerd, the progenitor of most of the Brainerd family in America. David's father, Hezekiah, was the seventh son and eighth child of Daniel."

* * *

As to the second group, Mr. Fuller writes:

NORTHAMPTON, MASSACHUSETTS

By your leave, Northampton hath a pleasant seat, as anyone with half an eye may see. This print in color was executed by J. B. Vinton and R. Sands in 1839. From the hotel porch you could view the chaste tower of the First Church of Christ in Northampton, erected by Isaac Damon in 1812, destroyed by fire in 1876. Of course, Jonathan Edwards did not preach in this edifice, the fourth home of the church. He preached in the third. The first meetings were in a log house, *circa* 1660; the second edifice was built 1670; the third, 1735, when Edwards' star was ascendant.

JONATHAN EDWARDS
HOUSE

PRESIDENT EDWARDS HOUSE, NORTHAMPTON, MASS.

Courtesy, the Library, Princeton University

As blunt old Cliff Lyman wrote, "The next thing after a bird in the hand is to get a cage for it." So—when young Mr. Edwards announced his engagement to Sarah Pierrepont, the "Mansion house, barn, and home lot of Mr. Sheldon" were purchased, May 1727, for 330 pounds. After their marriage, Jonathan and Sarah moved in. There the eleven children were born: Sarah, Jerusha, Esther, Mary, Lucy, Timothy, Susannah, Eunice, Jonathan, Elizabeth, and Pierrepont.

There also, October 9, 1747, David Brainerd died "in the lower parlor." (Right side of the picture.)

And the country round about Northampton! Here is Mount Tom! We would not omit the rainbow for any consideration. To us it is always there, for through the beautiful meadow David and Jerusha sometimes rode.

Mount Tom from the Northampton Meadows

From an old engraving by J. D. Woodward

"It consists of a few detached leaves containing entries for August 13-15, 1743; April 27, 1744; and January 29 and February 1 of an unidentified year."

* * *

By comparing the receipt in Brainerd's hand and signature, with the photostat of "Page 1" (both are shown in Packet 10) the author is convinced that Yale has fragments of the manuscript of the veritable Brainerd *Diary*. To be sure, Yale, with characteristic restraint, makes no such claim.

If Yale University would print, pamphlet form, both groups of manuscripts, it would confer a great gift upon the general public.

Now, the assumption that Jonathan Edwards disposed of the main body of Brainerd's *Diary,* is in no way affected by the Yale fragments. We esteem it a good fortune that Edwards did preserve a few fragments, and that we are able to reproduce one of them in this volume. But, by the large, when Edwards finished editing "David's precious papers," more sacred to him than to any of us, he *disposed of them.*

* * *

And by your leave, Edwards *did* edit! A critical analysis reveals that he blue-penciled with severity. For instance, Brainerd begins to enumerate the directions he gave the Kaunaumeek Indians for their migration to Stockbridge. Edwards crossed it off—"The particular manner has been omitted for brevity's sake."

Another reason for this severe editing was Edwards' sense of double responsibility. Out there in the Northampton cemetery were two lonely graves—one David's, the other Jerusha's. The pathetic entries in the *Memoirs* concerning their love for each

M

other were too sacred for the public eye. Sometimes Edwards was obliged to make casual reference, but he concealed it by generalization. For instance, when Jerusha rode down to Boston to nurse her dying sweetheart, Edwards wrote, "Brainerd was constantly attended by *one of my children* there."

The love letters of Jerusha to David came into Edwards' possession; likewise David's letters to Jerusha were found in Jerusha's effects after her death.

Sometimes, very discreetly, Edwards quotes from these love letters. Once he quotes a sentence from a typical boy-to-girl-after-getting-back-home-again letter—"I have had more pleasure this morning than all the drunkards in the world could enjoy!"

Edwards, however, sensed the fact that David's letters to Jerusha were somewhat formal; far more impersonal than his own letters to Sarah Pierrepont had been. Edwards' love letters were really good, not only before he married Sarah, but even after their family count stood at eleven, eight girls and three boys! He extenuates David's apparent detachment by commenting that David's letters "indicate affections in no ordinary degree chastened and spiritual."

"What about Jerusha's letters to David?"

Ah, well! Jerusha was just like her mother Sarah! She could— *no doubt did!*—write the kind of letters a man always keeps in a sacred place. But Edwards never let anyone see them. To her sorrowing father, Jerusha's letters belonged in the Ark of Lavender and Old Lace.

*   *   *

Another reason for Edwards' heavy editing was that he wrote to a purpose. He confessed that he slanted the quotations from the *Memoirs* to serve a propaganda end:

[The *Memoirs*] enable us to see not only how Brainerd spent his time from day to day, but also what passed in his heart . . . the value lies chiefly in the record of the ups and downs of his religious emotions.

So he edited to exhibit those "ups and downs." Every now and then he pries Brainerd's entries apart for comments:

The next few days he was comfortable, but immediately thereafter he complains about his sense of sin.

And Edwards' comments become very stereotyped indeed.

*   *   *

Brainerd's narrative is not in the least stereotyped—there is no real repetition in the *Memoirs*. His anguish for God, grief over a sinful nature, rapture derived from fleeting glimpses of divine glory, are conveyed in sentences as richly subtle and variant as symphony music. The boy was by nature and genius a word master, and had he chosen, he could have written deathless literature.

He knew that! Therein he had been greatly tempted—

Iniquity excited him to think of writing, that his name might live when he would be dead. Without desiring it, he found himself already possessed of [the power to write].

He never intended other eyes than his to see the *Memoirs;* but we would like to say to him, "David, *that* was no boast. We have never read any who excelled you in precision, force, or beauty of statement."

*   *   *

Yes, Edwards certainly edited! We know this because, by the large, the *Memoirs* lack the color we relished in *Trader Horn.* But Brainerd was color sensitive also. Now and then passages of pastel-beauty appear; there must have been many more. For example:

One evening, while his grief was greatest over the Yale disgrace, he felt some sweetness in the thoughts of arriving in a heavenly world. Suddenly, as he walked abroad [out-of-doors] the Northern Lights began to blaze in glory. If one has ever beheld this exhibition on a rare night in Canadian Summer, or while skating on Conover's pond, he will know what Brainerd meant—"I was delighted in contemplation on the glorious morning of the Resurrection."

He tells us about "the flat, nasal stab of a conk shell calling the tribes to assembly."

Arthur Tapping Pierson confessed how his blood ran cold when he read Brainerd's words about Susquehanna wolves howling at night about the campfire.

The sun was setting . . . he was safe in the home of his brother John . . . they sang the good songs of Zion . . . he was weak from his wearisome journey . . . but of a sudden his soul seemed to melt.

He draws aside the wigwam flap, and the reader sees him writing on "a divine subject by candle light a considerable time before dawn."

* * *

But Edwards' propaganda-editing was priceless. He was desirous that all ages should note Brainerd's total surrender to God, his continuous sense of personal unworthiness, his deathless devotion till death should set him free. Edwards' *Account* is one of faith's most powerful documents. Someone wrote, "Edwards' account of Brainerd's intense and pietistic life has blessed multitudes."

* * *

The reader of the *Memoirs* becomes deeply impressed by Brainerd's constant hunger for God, his passionate desire for total devotion, his yearning for Christlikeness—

"O that my soul might never offer any dead or cold services to my God!"

Certain entries, like the following, make it seem that Paul himself did not excel Brainerd in single-hearted devotion to God:

I've resolved that in my future ministry, I will not enter into other men's labors, neither will I settle down where the gospel was preached before. I will never make *that* my province! God has not given me liberty in that respect since I first decided to be a minister. I must gather a church for Him among the Indians, where no one has ever labored before. Ease and comfort shall never determine me!

* * *

Then, just as the reader is about to surrender his highest encomium to Brainerd, he is suddenly moved with aversion by such an entry as this:

I live so much of my time for nothing. . . . I do not desire to live for anything in this tiresome world. . . . I am not afraid to look the king of terrors in the face . . . afraid only if God leaves me. . . . I am impatient to be gone to Him. . . . But I'm willing to be from home as long as God sees fit. . . . O when will that happy day appear!

* * *

Thus you read on, admiring—disapproving, admiring—disapproving.

What, finally, will you do with the Flagellant David Brainerd? Neutral you cannot be. Either you will reject him as a hopeless extremist—in which case the upper lip will be curled above the canine tooth; or you will approve him, and resentment will utterly flee. In which case, your heart will be "bound with cords, even unto the horns of the altar."

XVIII

Mr. Edwards
Sets Up a Paradigm
(OCTOBER 5, 1703—OCTOBER 9, 1747)

We feel obliged to examine closely the life of a man whom Brainerd admired so much that his own life became a counterpart of the man he admired.

"He [Brainerd] detested enthusiasm in all its forms and operations, and condemned whatever in opinion or experience seemed to verge towards Antinomianism. He regarded with abhorrence the experiences of those whose first faith consists in believing that Christ died for them in particular; whose first love consists in loving God, because they suppose themselves the object of His love . . . and whose assurance of good estate rises from texts of Scripture that their sins are forgiven." (Edwards' Memorial Sermon preached at Brainerd's funeral, October 12, 1747)

Ah, Mr. Edwards, how naive your praise! It is just as if a virtuoso recorded his golden voice, then joined in the round of general applause when the record was run. But, Mr. Edwards, we know where Mr. Brainerd got his ideas!   (Sketch Book)

SO COMPLETELY DID EDWARDS'
life dominate Brainerd's that it
is necessary to know the former if the latter is to be understood.
Spurgeon so admired Puritan theology that his ultimate title seems
best expressed in *The Shadow of the Broad Brim*. But that influence came from a great company of men; it left Mr. Spurgeon
free to develop a personality of his own.

However, with Brainerd—if ever any single man, in due subordination to Christ, was permitted to be another's ideal—that's
what Edwards became to Brainerd. In fact, he out-Edwardsed
Edwards. Edwards admired the life of self-effacement; Brainerd
put a magnifying glass on Edwards' admiration—and *lived* it!

So, we give you Jonathan Edwards (October 5, 1703-March
22, 1758), whose career first shaped, and then whose eyes affectionately interpreted, the short, pathetic life of his counterpart,
David Brainerd.

*　　*　　*

Jonathan Edwards came of a good line. After all, isn't that
a good by-line for almost any New Englander? There was Richard E. Edwards, Jonathan's great-grandfather, a British clergyman;
William E. Edwards, his grandfather, a prosperous businessman
of Hartford; and Timothy E. Edwards, his father, a farmer-
preacher. Timothy married preacher Solomon Stoddard's daughter, Esther. Esther was a great blessing to Preacher Timothy, in
basket and store, as well as in giving him eleven children, all girls
save Jonathan; "sixty feet of daughters," each of the ten—so we

185

are reliably informed—well qualified for entrance in the Six Foot
Beauty Parade.

*   *   *

Surrounded by the older of the ten tall girls, the equally tall
and slender boy was off to an amazing start. He read Latin at
six, made incredible observations on the way of spiders at eleven.
At fourteen he read Newton and Locke "more greedily than
a miser gathering handfuls of gold."

At twelve he was a Yale student, able to read Latin, Greek,
and Hebrew, and possessed of a mind that cruised easily from
invisible atoms to enormously distant stars. . . . Yale days were
marked by thirteen hours of daily study, followed by rambles in
adjacent forests; and, a sustained contempt for any who were not
like Jonathan Edwards (i.e., thirteen hours a day of study, etc.).
In consequence, when this lanky, thin-lipped, sarcastic lad gradu-
ated at seventeen, "he had very few friends, and a growing repu-
tation for intellect."

At eighteen he became pastor of a little church in New York
City. Big Town then had about 12,000 population. The Hudson
River flowed out of a delightful wilderness, instead of the Bronx.
So woodland walks were continued along its banks. . . . At
twenty-one he was appointed a Yale tutor; at twenty-three he
became copastor with his grandfather, Solomon Stoddard, at
Northampton, Massachusetts.

Many interesting details of Colonial life must, as Edwards
would have said, "be omitted for brevity's sake." But as an
example, take the matter of diet: The people rose at sunrise; they
ate a breakfast of bread and milk, or bread and cider, with a cornmeal pudding. Then they worked in the fields. At noon, a good
roast, and some more pudding. In the fields again until night-

fall, then supper—cold meat and bread and milk. And if you wished, you could top off with some cold cornmeal pudding. . . .

* * *

When Solomon Stoddard died in 1728, Jonathan became sole pastor. His printed sermons quickly began to circulate over New England; they were eagerly read by the Colonial intelligentsia, and even shipped to Europe!

July 28, 1727, Jonathan married Sarah, daughter of James Pierrepont and his third wife, Mary Hooker. Pierrepont was a New Haven pastor, and a cofounder and trustee of Yale University. Sarah, a bride at seventeen, was thus described: "As good as she was beautiful, and as beautiful as she was good." She did equally as well by Jonathan as Jonathan's mother, Esther, did by his father. Sarah bore Jonathan eleven children, the second of whom was Jerusha. And Jerusha was her mother all over again.*

* * *

In September, 1743, Edwards at forty had come to full honors. He and Benjamin Franklin were recognized by Europeans as "the first Americans having any kinds of intellects at all." He was invited to deliver the Yale Baccalaureate Sermon. In the audience sat Brainerd, "then in disgrace." Of course, Brainerd had heard Edwards speak before; and for most of his conscious life Edwards had been to him the pole star of everything worth while. But

---

* This fecundity, as well as intellectuality, seems to have been passed down in the family. Nine of the Edwards children (two were unmarried) presented Jonathan and Sarah with *seventy-two grandchildren!* The unmarried girls were Jerusha and Elizabeth (May 6, 1747—January 1, 1762). Sarah (August 25, 1728) bore Elihu Parsons eleven children. Esther (February 13, 1732) bore Aaron Burr two children. Mary (April 7, 1734) bore Timothy Dwight thirteen children. Lucy (August 31, 1736) bore Jakael Woodbridge seven children. Susannah (June 20, 1740) bore Eleazer Porter five children. Eunice (May 9, 1743) bore Thomas Pollock five children. Of the boys, Timothy (July 25, 1738) had fifteen children; Jonathan (May 26, 1745) had four children; Pierrepont (April 8, 1750) had ten children.

this time it was different. This time he met and formed a personal
acquaintance with Mr. Edwards.

But that was not all. Edwards' second daughter, Jerusha, accompanied him, horseback, from Northampton to Boston; and
the church paid all her expenses. And on this notable day, David
met—Jerusha, too! In his forest walk that September evening
(just like Mr. Edwards), the joys of the day made the burden
of his expulsion from Yale seem far lighter. He even felt elated.
How excellent was Mr. Edwards. And Jerusha . . . !

We must tell you a little more. Not long after, Brainerd rode
over to Northampton to confer with Mr. Edwards about his expulsion from Yale. But we must be honest. That was not the
only reason.

*   *   *

Thus was consummated a formative friendship—Paul and
Timothy revised for Colonial Days. Everything about the whole
affair was a joy to Edwards' heart. He was aware that David was
emulating him. David was himself all over again. It seemed
good that David and Jerusha were so interested in each other.
Jerusha was Sarah all over again. . . . In fact, it seemed as if he,
Jonathan Edwards, and Sarah Pierrepont, in the persons of David
Brainerd and Jerusha Edwards, were starting all over again!
Edwards often looked out his study window towards Mount Tom
and mused over the matter.

*   *   *

Ah, I nearly forgot my obligations as a stolid historian. . . .
Let me see: we were to set forth how Edwards influenced Brainerd.

Well, you can see it in the matter of Edwards' conversion.
At eighteen, Edwards came under conviction, after a painful

struggle in which the sovereignty of God was uppermost. The idea that as Sovereign, God had a full right to elect all men, before they were born, to eternal bliss or eternal damnation, forced Edwards to realize there was nothing he could do about it. He did, for a time, try moral improvement as a means to God's favor; but he finally gave it up: "he was lost"! This surrender did not make him happy, but at least he felt less distraught than when he was struggling.

Suddenly, without his even thinking about his own salvation, his soul was overwhelmed with an abstract sense of the beauty of God.

Rejoicing over this "inner light," he looked again at the doctrine of Sovereignty. What a change! He formerly "hated the thought; now he loved it, even though he was lost"! And then, as an effulgent aftermath, he suddenly realized he was saved. There was no text associated with his experience. It was just the appearance of "an inner light." At once he felt it was necessary for everyone else to get saved the same way as he had. There was no importance attached to any text. The *summum bonum* should be an "inner light." It is striking that Brainerd, when twenty-two and already an avid reader of Edwards, had the same experience. More striking still, that when the Indians at Crossweeksung became Christians, their account of it was just like Brainerd's. "Not think any thing 'bout self: just how good God is." Thus the Indians became, in effect, theological grandchildren of Edwards.

*   *   *

In 1734 Edwards somewhat codified his views upon the way to salvation, as he saw it in his own conversion: "A Devine [sic] and Spiritual Light *Immediately Imparted* to the Soul by the Spirit of God." The best assurance of salvation was this "devine light," a spiritual joy attending an effusion of God's beauty on the soul. This "spiritual joy," which amounted to "intuitive awareness," was a man's sufficient, if not exclusive, proof that he had become a saved creature. Salvation assurance was entirely intrinsic, never in the slightest, extrinsic.

Brainerd devoured that sermon. It is interesting to note that his own conversion is a duplicate of Edwards'. You may now re-read the chapter "Dark Grove: Unspeakable Glory" with a fuller understanding. . . . It was Edwards' all over again.

Edwards' analysis of regeneration, based on his own experience, carried him to very unhappy conclusions: "the proof of salvation being an inner light, and not some Bible text, excluded dependence upon the thought that 'Christ died for me personally.' " And Brainerd's complete acceptance of this idea led him to make statements in the *Memoirs* which are tinged with the "party spirit" which he so greatly disliked, and which the reader wishes had never been recorded.

*   *   *

Similarly, it is possible to trace Brainerd's *staples* of doctrine, as well as his doctrinal *skews and biases,* right back to Jonathan Edwards. Of the staples—

1. Concerning the Shorter Catechism—found blameless! "Mr. Brainerd, the way you speak of that code, we are often puzzled as to whether you regard it a superlative human interpretation of revelation, or revelation itself. For our part, we admire it; but we will never bind it with the Bible."

2. Concerning the doctrine of original sin—Brainerd was never misled by the idea that "there is a spark of divine fire burning in the souls of men, needing only to be fanned." All a man had to do to be convinced that all fell in Adam, was to look into his own heart: there he would see the fountain of sin.

3. Concerning the Holy Spirit—he had no time for such folly as that. He was to be considered merely an emanation of God—a sort of vaporous excretion, on the order of that which enables a horse to scent his owner. Nonsense! The Holy Spirit is a *Person,* "propagating at once experimental and speculative knowledge."

4. Concerning Baptism and the Lord's Supper—these were golden candlesticks given by God for arresting the interest of sinner and saint alike. . . .

So the inventory could continue. The emphasis upon sturdy fundamentals in Brainerd's divinity was singularly Edwardsian in sentiment and statement.

Of the slants and tilts of doctrine—the humanly derived second cousins of revelation!—those things which might, and often do, become the dangerous heresies of Christianity—

1. As to the true ends of salvation—a Christian must never seek to get to heaven, instead of somewhere else, for his own advantage; neither, having arrived, is his joy to center upon his own blessed estate! Never! His purpose is always to glorify God! "Well, how about *'enjoying* Him forever,' Mr. Brainerd? That too is catechistical." One is not to think of his own good fortune: he is to think of nought else save glorifying God. "Well, Mr. Brainerd, *that* is a degree of spiritual discipline which we never expect to attain. Your idea may not become dangerous, but it is too much leftist of Flagellantism to be sane, practical, or desirable. . . . Yet, that is one of the things which made you David Brainerd, instead of John Doe!"

2. As to salvation by grace *exclusively*—guard that idea! it is a dangerous doctrine. Mr. Edwards was fearful about the reality of his own salvation, if it were animated solely by his tongue (textual proof). He felt safe only if his salvation were animated by religious work and discipline. Antinomians are bad company! "Now *that*, Mr. Brainerd, is heresy, and such thinking has spawned the ugly hobgoblins which today infest Modernism. . . . How did you ever overlook the text, 'Not of works, lest any man should boast'?"

3. As to how one may know he is saved—well, the proof is the joyous impression God's power and beauty makes upon you. That is what Mr. Edwards always taught. "Well, Mr. Brainerd, for our part, we will never let Mr. Edwards' dictums displace the Word and the Testimony."

There, in main, were the facts and foibles received and re-emphasized in Brainerd through the media of his warm admiration of Edwards.

* * *

Certain of the perils in Edwards' biases were finally exposed in his own pastorate. In 1734, his sermon "Justification by Faith" was attested by six surprising conversions. Conversions for a time thereafter came frequently. Finally there were thirty a week!

The somewhat cold Mr. Edwards set up an Inquiry Room! He became as much a psychological expert as Ignatius Loyola. The matter upon which he put the high premium was "a proper admiring awe" in the seeker after God.

"Do you now possess that proper admiring awe?" he insisted, as he dealt with the converts.

To make certain of this awe, he codified his tests of conversion:

1. Do you recognize your guilt as a God-hater? (If God were in your reach, you would endeavor to do away with him in an hour! That can be demonstrated.)
2. Are you submissive to the fact that you already are condemned, and can do nothing about it? (That, too, can be demonstrated.)
3. Having become submissive, do you possess a disinterested adoration of the mercy of God, followed by a heavenly frame? That (not a Scripture) is the proof of your salvation. (That can never be demonstrated. "Faith cometh by hearing, and hearing by the word of God."—*Romans 10:17.*)

* * *

McGiffert "stated the case better than he knew":

"The great awakening with which Mr. Edwards was associated saw through the speciousness that a man's claim on life is satisfied when he

JONATHAN EDWARDS AND YALE

Courtesy of Yale University Art Gallery

JONATHAN EDWARDS
Painted by Joseph Badger

As a preacher, he never raved. He mounted the Tower of the Flock, "venerated for his saintliness, hated for his pitiless assaults on pretenders," and just talked. There he stood, tall—six feet, one inch of him—slender, delicate of constitution, slightly effeminate, large eyed, a soft voice, pathos saturated. In his left hand, his sermon notes, written in a smallish book; with his right hand he turned pages. Strangers at first thought, "Not much fight in that preacher." A little later, "Well, there's a man who will never run when the Devil says, 'Boo!'" And finally, as Edwards got down to Sinners in the Hands of an Angry God, their consciences cried, "There's a lethal punch in that soft voice."

YALE UNIVERSITY—AERIAL VIEW

We could see the fabulous campus of Yale University. "Yale and Prince-ton!" I thought. "Those very names gladden the American heart." They are different, to be sure. Yale may be classified as Knowledge tempered by Faith; Princeton as Faith tempered by Knowledge. But Jonathan Edwards, Graduate of the former and President of the latter, was as a vinculum for joining the two.

•

The Sterling Divinity Quadrangle cannot be seen in the aerial view above. Just beyond the entrance to the Quadrangle, at 409 Prospect Place, stands the David Brainerd House. It bears the amazing inscription, "David Brainerd, Class of 1743." By this inscription and in many other ways, it would seem that the University has confessed her errors and paid tribute to the greatness of Brainerd's total career.

DAVID BRAINERD HOUSE, YALE UNIVERSITY
DIVINITY SCHOOL, STERLING DIVINITY QUADRANGLE

Photos,
Courtesy of
Yale University
News Bureau

becomes a good citizen. [So far, good.] Religion was more than civics. [Also, good.] It was the profoundly stirring response and reconstruction of an individual's whole nature, in the face of *impressions of power, beauty, and goodness which God made upon him.* [And *that* is the birth-place of Modernism.]"

* * *

In a few months the revival died. People struggling for this "inner light" began to contemplate suicide. Edwards said, "Satan took control." All of which gives much interest in John Jasper's corn-bread canon: "If you ain't restin' on Scripture, Brudder, de Debbil will get you sure!"

N

XIX

And Edits
an Autobiography

(1749)

Herein we enter a library in Northampton, Massachusetts, and contemplate a sorrowing father who is "carving a book" from the Memoirs *of the young man to whom his daughter was engaged. He titles the new book,* An Account of the Life of David Brainerd; *but he could with propriety have titled it,* An Extension of the Life of Jonathan Edwards. *For Brainerd was Edwards all over again, a sort of khaki edition of a Morocco classic.*

Edwards "nauseated noisy religion." Faith must wear sneakers when it walked abroad. The Yale fiasco burned this into Brainerd's soul. He repeated the idea with underscore, never patient with anything like "party spirit" in himself or anyone else. Such persons needed to be "chastened with briars and thorns."

Edwards deprecated "ignorant, untrained men in the pulpit" (laymen in particular). That prejudice abounds in Brainerd.

Edwards felt that salvation proof was not a matter of texts, but of a heavenly frame. Brainerd went his mentor one better:

"Could not but think, as I have often remarked to others, that much more of true religion consists in deep humility, brokenness of heart, and an abasing sense of barrenness and want of grace and holiness, than most who are called Christians, imagine; especially those who have been esteemed the converts of the late day. Many seem to know of no other religion but elevated joys and affections, arising only from some flights of imagination, or some suggestion made to their mind, of Christ being theirs, God loving them, and the like. Antinomianism diminishes the necessity of holiness of life, and abates man's regard to the commands of God."   (Memoirs)

T HE DEATH OF EDWARDS' GRANDFATHER, Solomon Stoddard, was the occasion of Edwards becoming pastor *de facto* of the Northampton Church. He immediately addressed himself to an abuse which the "tall, dignified old Pope Solomon" had introduced—unregenerate church membership. That abuse developed as follows: Stoddard (1643-1728) attended a Synod in 1662, when the "Half Way Covenant" was first proposed; "persons not sufficiently advanced in grace for full membership in the Church could secure membership for their babies" (who were not advanced at all). Stoddard liked the idea, and added to it: "Professing Christians who were not sure, should be permitted to *take communion.*" Then he improved it still more: "People may become *members* on a profession of faith, no affirmation of experience necessary." All of which reminds us of Gilbert and Sullivan's sparkling ditty, "Here's a Pretty Howdy-Do!"

* * *

There's no attempt here to bemean Pastor Stoddard. Did he not have five great revivals?—the first in 1669 when he was the new pastor; the last in 1718, when at seventy-five he was the venerable shepherd? Did he not write a tract, *A Guide to Christ,* which was a great blessing to Brainerd when he was a seeker after God? And was he not "sternly opposed to *excessive* [sic] drinking, long hair, wigs, and fancy wardrobes?"

Nevertheless, the church membership at Northampton filled up with members between whom and stark worldings there was

197

not a hair's breadth of difference. That always means trouble;
and Jonathan Edwards inherited the trouble. As soon as the old
man died, Edwards declared war on Half Way Ideals. He saw con-
ditions in Northampton were bad, very, very bad, even in the
church. The complacent eyes of grandfather had become so poor
he couldn't see what was going on under his own nose. Church
members were attending "frolics." In 1949 these frolics would
classify as fast-moving Hollywood studio parties.

There was also bundling, a distinctive New England contribution to the social disorder: "Young people of different sexes
(fully clothed, to be sure) lay in bed together." Charles Francis
Adams sneered, "The very bundling was done by the hands of
mothers and sisters." Certain church members themselves were
enthusiastic bundlers. Of course, extenuation was offered: "New
England houses were cold in the winter. Young folks had to keep
company." To all of which Edwards' comment, translated a la
George Ade, was, "Now, who's kidding whom?"

Edwards did not rave over bundling. As a preacher, he
never raved. He mounted the Tower of the Flock, "venerated for
his saintliness, hated for his pitiless assaults on pretenders," and
talked. There he stood, tall, slender, delicate of constitution,
slightly effeminate, large eyed; his soft voice, pathos saturated. In
his left hand he held his sermon notes, written in a smallish book;
with his right hand he turned pages. Strangers thought at first,
"Not much fight in that preacher." A little later, "Well, there's
a man who will never run when the Devil says 'Boo!'" And
finally, as Edwards got down to "Sinners in the hands of an angry
God," their consciences cried, "There's a lethal punch in that
soft voice."

"The young people of Northampton were constantly on [Pastor
Edwards'] mind. He thought the younger generation was going

to perdition, and he did not cease telling them so. . . . Edwards was a perfectionist . . . severe in moral demands he made upon his parishioners; no less upon himself . . . a hard taskmaster, ill content with careless living" (McGiffert). The anguish, therefore, of carnal churchmen who ran wild when Edwards got down to preaching, justified one of McGiffert's chapter titles, "The Sacred Gadfly of Northampton."

At this point, Edwards became involved in a type of bundling all his own. He publicly announced a sort of findings committee in which without discrimination he bundled the names of bundlers and nonbundlers. Thus he provided the opposition with a fine red herring for dragging over the trail. . . . On June 22, 1750, the church voted upon the recommendation of his dismissal as pastor. "Two hundred arms flew up as if on springs [bundle springs?], and twenty voted to retain him."

* * *

Our eyes are now trained upon the unemployed minister with a wife and ten children. (Jerusha died in 1748.) And one of the ten was the baby boy, Pierrepont, two months old. Brainerd, too, is dead; he and Jerusha lie buried in the cemetery down by the bridge. There were weeks of terrible privations for the family. "The girls had to make fans to sell in Boston." Poor Edwards wept his grief out in a letter to John Erskine of Edinburgh, Scotland: "What shall I do? I am thrown upon a wide ocean of the world, and know not what will become of me and my numerous family." After certain hungry months, he received a signal demotion. John Sergeant died, 1749, and Edwards accepted a call to "the little church, mixed Indian and white," up in the Berkshires. It looked bad.

That is to say, it *looked* bad, but "God moves in a mysterious way His wonders to perform." When David Brainerd died in the Northampton parsonage, October 9, 1747, Edwards came into possession, as before noted, of Brainerd's papers, his *Memoirs,* and the like. New Englanders urged Edwards to write Brainerd's biography. This task was most congenial to Edwards, for Brainerd, curiously, was "a justification of the kind of religion Edwards had always pleaded for." It was wonderful to write a book which would in telling about Brainerd become a carom-shot approval of the author himself.

So he wept through "dear David's pitiful papers, the most melancholy person he ever met," editing the day by day entries, and from time to time interpolating comments of his own.

As he wrote, Edwards was at first mindful of the boy who *imitated* him. Then he saw how much more gloriously the boy had lived than he. One day he thought, "There's just one thing to be done now: I must imitate David!" At about this time the "demotion" came. But it was not demotion at all! Dear David had made such a romance of his self-effacement among the Indians! Now he, Edwards, would do the same in Stockbridge. With a strangely warmed heart he moved to Stockbridge, August 8, 1751, David in view; just as David is in your view, good Flock of the Pages. And over in the Berkshire Hills, with David in view, Edwards sealed his position as a master of good English prose, and a top figure in American theology, by writing such books as *The Freedom of the Will.*

In the year 1758, John Brainerd and Caleb Smith, both trustees of the College of New Jersey, rode up to Stockbridge, authorized to offer Edwards the Presidency. . . . He accepted . . . but in a few weeks died. . . . However, you have herein the clue which suggested asking Princeton if it had Brainerd's Hebrew Lexicon.

What a picture could be made of this near-tragedy! The heartbreak of a minister being discharged in the line of doing his duty! The numerous Edwards family moving into a backwoods parish!

But under this picture let us set this text:

"They prevented me in the day of my calamity: but the Lord was my stay. He brought me forth also into a large place: he delivered me, because he delighted in me."—*II Samuel 22:19-20.*

XX

Indian Summer

(JULY 1, 1745—MARCH 20, 1747)

Several reasons appear which make it seem necessary to Brainerd to double his missionary labors, as his life is ending—or perhaps it would be better to say, thus ending his life.

"Indian Summer" is a bejewelled phrase two words long, strictly American, and destined to sparkle forever on the outstretched finger of English literature. It indicates "those halcyon days," as De Quincy called them, which appear several weeks before the December solstice, and which are reputed to have power to hold blizzards off at arm's length so that nature may accomplish certain things "e'er the winter's storms begin."

The Halcyon was a bird, much resembling his American cousin the Kingfisher. Tradition said the Halcyon made a floating sea-nest in late October or early November, and that this structure had great mastery over turbulent waters. During the two weeks in which the fledglings matured, this mysterious nest not only held back the riotous billows, but extended the benison shoreward, so that the labors of men on shore might receive a golden-houred finale before the night cometh when no man can work.

(Sketch Book)

NDOUBTEDLY THE COURSE OF action upon which Brainerd decided, July 1, 1745, was the means of swiftly ending his life. He determined, no matter what sacrifice and travail were involved, to devote ruthlessly to the service of God whatever "little inch of life he had remaining":

I am God's Pilgrim Hermit. I will spend my life to my last moment in caves and dens of the earth, if the kingdom of Christ may be thereby advanced.

* * *

That decision was virtually suicide. . . . What moved upon him to make such a committal? There were certain reasons perfectly logical to him, three of which are hereby listed, just as he stated them:

1. Throughout his work "he had always complained that his labors were barren" (Edwards). His ministry was not the power it ought to be. Up to July 1, 1745, after three years on the field, he *had not baptized a single convert!* Perhaps he should resign his commission. He would give himself one more trial. He would *really* devote himself to his task, and if by November 20 nothing worthy were accomplished, he would discontinue as a missionary.

2. The great interest which developed within a few days after the beginning of the work at Crossweeksung seemed to indicate that the Spirit was about to "trouble the waters," not only in New Jersey, but everywhere among the Indian peoples. It would be tragic—he could never forgive himself!—if in this day of

visitation he failed to redeem the time, whatever the cost to him personally.

3. The last reason which forced the living sacrifice decision, was his acute and mounting sense of personal sin and vileness. Just what was that sin?

The *Memoirs* bristle with hints of it, and consequent macabre self-judgments. Readers of the *Memoirs* at first try to dismiss the matter by thinking, "It all arises from the boy's anguish over his expulsion from Yale." But the time comes when this explanation no longer avails. After his grief had hardened into apathy, and the smart of the college disgrace was deadened by time, the *Memoirs* still abound in references to sin in his life.

On April 17, 1747, two days before he left New Jersey for the last time, he made an entry which explains everything; an entry which relieves every dark misgiving we might have entertained hitherto:

> Could not but rejoice that ever God should discover His reconciled face to such a vile sinner as myself. . . . Shame and confusion at times covered me . . . I could not but admire the divine goodness, *that the Lord had not let me fall into the grossest, vilest acts of sin and open scandal that could be thought of,* and felt so much necessitated to praise God, that this was ready for a little while to swallow up my shame on account of my sins.

The mystery is resolved! It is a repetition of the ancient anguish of Christians over "bodies awaiting redemption"! the same self-condemnation of white saints like Paul, who have cried, "O miserable man that I am!" Not that Brainerd ever *yielded;* but had not God helped, it was in him to do it. We need never know the specifications of Brainerd's temptations. What any man may find in his own heart should bar curiosity from trying to ferret out what troubled Brainerd. . . . But to Brainerd, this evidence

of guilt, and this mercy of God which delivered him, constituted
the loftiest argument for complete devotion—

> "Had I a thousand hearts to give,
> Lord, they should all be Thine."

* * *

July 1 he launched the new life of total self-immolation. He
concluded he must immediately return to the Forks of the Delaware.* He left the work at Crossweeksung under the charge of
William Tennent. En route, July 10, Fautaury remarked to him,
"When I get home on the Delaware, my wife and I wish to be
baptized." So here was to be his first trophy of grace. The new
devotion was already being rewarded!

Brainerd at this point made the longest single entry in the
Memoirs. It covers three and a half printed pages in Edwards'
Account, so it is appropriate to present a digest of it here.

Fautaury's life was the substance of romance. Born in the
Delaware River forests about 1705, his tall figure as a boy early
attracted the attention of white settlers. They were pleased with
his amiability, honesty, dependability. He swiftly mastered the
English language and became a traders' interpreter. As a hand-
some young brave, he married a beautiful Minnehaha of the
Tepees. Two children were born. But it must be written, Fautaury fell a victim to White Man's Fire Water. He did not become a besotted creature. He retained many fine graces, but from
time to time went on "uproarious drunks."

In June, 1744, Brainerd employed Fautaury as his interpreter.
The arrangement was not entirely satisfactory, because Fautaury
was unfamiliar with Christian ideals and terminology. To in-

---

* Once again it seems necessary to remind the reader that the Forks of the Delaware were
always a part of his field of labor, his commission reading, "Delaware and Susquehanna
Indians." He did not give up Sakhauwotung when he went to Crossweeksung.

crease his mastery of English, Fautaury attended an English gospel service. There he first came under conviction.

"But he declined . . . late autumn he again came under deep conviction." At this point Brainerd spent a whole night interceding for him. Fautaury said next day, "I give my heart to Jesus." Then his wife made the same statement; then the two children confessed faith.

Brainerd did not feel justified in baptizing them until they gave full assurance of regeneration. The moral change in Fautaury, however, was a forest miracle. He was instantly and permanently freed from liquor. He attached himself to Brainerd with unusual devotion. When he interpreted Brainerd's sermons, he became as responsive to Brainerd's frames as a violin is to the virtuoso. Brainerd wrote:

When I was favored with more than common freedom, fervency, or power, Fautaury was affected in the same manner. . . . The faces of the whole Indian assembly would be changed. Tears and sobs became common.

*   *   *

July 21 the Fautaurys were baptized; July 26, the children. The ordinance had a powerful effect—

Divine truth made a considerable impression. Seeing the interpreter and his family baptized brought great concern among the Indians for their own souls.

Yes, God was working on the Delaware too! The night of July 26, Brainerd made a significant entry:

This is a golden time for the work of God: even White Heathen are awakened. . . . If he were but more diligent, this revival would appear everywhere . . . he longed that his little inch of life might be filled with more activity in the things of God . . . he desired an angel's vigor and ardor.

Packet 13

SUSQUEHANNA VIEWS

"Even to this day there is a glory in the Susquehanna which civilization has not stamped out. The majestic water- and landscapes enable the mind to overlook today's barges which, like giant black hogs, grunt and puff for coal beneath the currents. We do not marvel that from earliest days Europe and America sent their best artists into this wilderness to sketch its glories."

VIEW OF SUNBURY, PENNSYLVANIA, FROM MILE HILL
THE SITE OF ANCIENT OPELHAUPUNG

Two of the
Wayfarers:
Deborah and
Queen Elizabeth

See page 13

SUNBURY, PENNSYLVANIA. VIEW FROM BLUE HILL

Brainerd's joy was increased when he returned to Crossweeksung. Under the ministry of Tennent, the work had grown in power. The Indians were journeying thirty miles to receive instruction at Tennent's parsonage in Freehold. Everywhere the Day Star seemed to rise in glory.

* * *

The reasons just listed that drove Brainerd to a life of utter flagellantism, and the apparently immediate results of this life, now forced him to make a decision that he had contemplated in the Delaware wilderness. He wondered if he were not obliged to forswear that which was dearest to himself and become a recluse for God—a Pilgrim Hermit!

This idea and this terminology suddenly appear in his thinking as early as July 31, 1744. In a letter to Jerusha under that date he wrote:

I love to be a pilgrim and stranger in this wilderness. It seems fit for such a poor, ignorant, worthless, despised creature as I.

Later, as the idea developed, he added the words "hermit"—suggesting celibacy, instead of "stranger."

* * *

However, during the opening months at Crossweeksung, he had not as yet sensed the conclusions to which his thinking was driving him—

In June, at Crossweeksung he felt *he should settle down there* as pastor. Settling down meant a fireside of his own—with Jerusha!

He wrote her a letter on this point, with a warmth unusual for him.

o

But within a few days, the terrible logic of his own thinking overwhelmed him:

He was peculiarly trained and fitted to be God's Pilgrim Hermit—and that made him say with Job, "All my plans are broken off!"
He wrote Jerusha a letter as tragic as any man ever wrote to his woman. . . .
I am constrained, yet chose, to say "Farewell" . . . friends and earthly comforts, the dearest of them all, *the very dearest* . . . adieu, adieu! . . . I will spend my life to my last moments, in caves and dens of the earth, if the Kingdom of Christ may thereby be advanced.

* * *

Thereupon he poured into his work for the next twenty-one months the last measure of blood and tears. He wrote, December 2, 1745, that he had doubled his diligence in his Master's service. And that was precisely what he had done.

* * *

Poignantly aware that the night was falling, he increased his labors in the gospel. Three powerful considerations moved upon him—the great awakening at Crossweeksung, his own physical condition, and "the mysterious constraint of Love Divine." As to the first, the Crossweeksung revival might be the omen of the Day of Visitation among the Indian tribes; and, if that were the case, the King's business required haste. As to the second, he was convinced his own life was nearing the end; whatever he could do he must do quickly. And, as to the third, his sense of gratitude to God for showing His reconciled face to one so sinful as himself, persuaded him that he was not his own; he was bought with a price! He *must* work for the night was falling!

The night was falling, indeed! Therefore, he was constantly in the saddle, agonizing his way from one wigwam village to another. The infesting afreets, anguish of body and anxiety of mind rode constantly with him. Now and then he lifted his pale face and murmured, "O God! there is no rest but in Thee!" Even the Narragansett pony was moved upon by the travail in the man's soul. She turned her head toward her rider and nickered softly. Of this mysterious tribute from brute creation, no one but a hard-pressed horseman may know.

*　　*　　*

The diligence he gave in the first thirty-one months of his work does not seem capable of being doubled. In that time, November 25, 1742, to July 1, 1745, he rode in the line of duty, 7500 miles! To be sure, his work was not riding; but riding constitutes a fair scale for representing labor involved. Would it be possible to double such labors?

In the writing of biography, I have felt it necessary to build a trellis of the subject's life, a day-by-day analysis. In Brainerd's trellis, the overall total of his horseback mileage comes to around 15,000 miles. Small wonder McGiffert said, "Brainerd was motor-minded." His average yearly riding exceeded that of Francis Asbury! He often rode as much as fifty miles a day; once— seventy-five! To allay doubt as to the possibility of riding such distance in a pioneer land, James Fenimore Cooper wrote, "The American forests admit of the passage of a horse, there being little underbrush, and few tangled brakes."

*　　*　　*

Of course 15,000 miles does not seem excessive to an auto age. But the map grows great if one envisions the state of early America! stones, fallen logs! cold and snow! rain and oceans of mud! sultry summer and choking dust! . . .

Let us break our figures down to see if he actually doubled his labors. Since he rode a total of 15,000 miles, 7500 in his first *thirty-one* months; it is evident he rode another 7500 miles in his last *twenty-one* months. *But, during five months of the last twenty-one he was confined to his bed!* This looks so much like doubling, that no honest man will care to cavil.

* * *

The trellis reveals also that in the fulfillment of his vow, he made twenty-eight tiresome side journeys. . . . Once his horse was stolen, and he was obliged to walk for several days. Once he preached every night for a week, while riding the eighty miles from the Forks of the Delaware to Crossweeksung. . . . But on he went—Connecticut Farms, Staten Island, Elizabeth Town, Allen's Town, Long Island, Newark, Kingston, Freehold, Philadelphia, and the last two trips to the Susquehanna River!

In addition, he rode 3000 miles in pastoral calling at Crossweeksung . . . he began to preach "double services.". . . To John he wrote:

"I am in one continual, perpetual, and uninterrupted hurry."

In the *Memoirs*: "My labors are as great as my nature will permit."

* * *

It is to be doubted if anything in literature excels the record of the devotion which Brainerd offered as he labored in the fiery heat of his Indian Summer; as he applied himself to the King's business; as he toiled before the season of grace should end!

As a result, his body was burned to a cinder. He painfully made his way back to Northampton to *die* in the *home of his sweetheart's father,* when—may these lines be forgiven!—he might have *lived* with her in *their own home!*

But, we must remember, this is the Life Story of a Flagellant.

XXI

The Susquehanna,
River of Frustration

(OCTOBER 2-12, 1744; MAY 8-30, 1745; SEPTEMBER 9-28,
1745; AUGUST 12—SEPTEMBER 20, 1746)

*An account of four journeys and four defeats
in the Susquehanna wilderness, the last of
which, particularly, completely broke the health
of the missionary, and swiftly brought his life
to a close.*

Three times Brainerd's compassion for the Susquehanna Indians impelled him to cross the wilderness between Easton, Pennsylvania, and the area where modern Sunbury is located. Each trip exacted a heavy toll in physical strength; and each trip was a signal disappointment. A fourth time he felt he must go: his Pilgrim Hermit vow demanded it.

But this ride was with death—and he knew it. He had become too frail to cross the mountains, so he rode to the Susquehanna by the low level route—via Philadelphia and the Chesapeake Bay.

And there, at last, we found him . . . the coal towers of modern Pennsylvania melted away, the forests of yesterday and the ancient Indian village of Opelhaupung returned, and the Man himself appeared. But I saw he was dying. He coughed incessantly, his body was shockingly thin, his cheeks sunken. All my flippant aversion for him now shrank back ashamed. I saw he had paid Greater Love's great price, and thus he deserved acclamation as one of the Great Hearts of the Faith. (Sketch Book)

VERILY, THE APPOSITION OF THIS chapter title will seem libelous to those who love the Susquehanna—an attitude which we, too, share. For we have come to cherish this goodly American river, from the Chesapeake Bay to Northumberland, Pennsylvania; from thence, on the West Branch to the Alleghany Mountains, on the madly writhing course. And from Northumberland along the serene curves of the North Branch to Otsego Lake, in New York—"Glimmerglass," as Cooper called it. There, at Cooperstown, you will find shrines to Baseball, Old Furniture, and the statue of the author of *The Leather-stocking Tales.*

Even to this day there is a glory in the Susquehanna which civilization has not stamped out. The majestic water- and land-scapes enable the mind to overlook today's barges which, like giant black hogs, grunt and puff for coal beneath the currents. We do not marvel that from earliest days Europe and America sent their best artists into this wilderness to sketch its glories.

* * *

But to Brainerd, the Susquehanna meant frustration, just as it did to the Pantisocrats, Southey, Coleridge, and Lovel. Even as the dreams of those poets of a heaven on the Susquehanna frayed into tear-faded threads, so Brainerd's hopes for the evangelization of the River Indians were broken off.

* * *

Inasmuch as the Susquehanna proved to be such a heartbreak to Brainerd, we resolved to see it for ourselves, to duplicate his anguished journeys through the wilderness. . . . Now, when we read his memo of wolves howling about the night camp, we are again in hilly Pottsville, where modern wolves howl around a hot-dog stand. . . . And when we recall his pained comment upon the profanity of Dutch traders at Paxtang, we think of traffic jams near the east end of the Pennsylvania Turnpike.

*   *   *

The wilderness which two hundred years ago stood between Easton and Sunbury, then stretched on to Altoona, must have conveyed a sense of majestic solitude. Rand McNally's road map suggests the broken character of this country by the mass of striation lines, representing mountain ranges which curve for two hundred miles in parallel formation, like giant rainbows.

In Brainerd's day, wild life abounded, wolves, bears, deer, and bobcats. Picturesque streams, like the Juniata, the Schuylkill, the Lehigh, and the Tobihanna, drained the dark valleys which lay between the hills.

John James Audubon lingered for weeks during the summer of 1829 in Northeastern Pennsylvania, drawing such remarkable birds as the Canada Fly Catcher, the Pine Swamp Warbler, and the Black and Yellow Warbler. Even today, men who refuse to let gold dust and sheep's wool blind their eyes, will find as much to admire in Northeastern Pennsylvania as in the High Sierras of Northern California.

As a matter of fact, these Pennsylvania mountains were anciently just as high as the Sierras, but nature pushed huge glaciers over their tops, grinding them down; afterwards she carpeted the slopes with long lines of pines filing upwards, interspersed with deciduous forest beauties—Oaks, Maples, Butternuts. No part of the United States has, for the Cedar-Palms Wayfarers, charms exceeding those of Northeastern Pennsylvania.

The ancient Red Men left behind them place names which persist to this day—Mauch Chunk, Shaumoking, and Tamaqua. Pious early settlers, too, left place names such as Eschol, Bethlehem, and Mt. Carmel.

But the pristine glory of the Keystone State has departed. Coal towers, like evil steel fungi, have crumbled many of the ancient forests, of which occasional clumps of Maple, Thorn, Butternut, or Sycamores are melancholy witness; while Rhododendrons, Goldenrod, and Sassafras spell out the "Ichabods" of the wilderness.

* * *

In July, 1744, certain Indians at the Forks of the Delaware told Brainerd of an Indian hunting party camped out in the wilderness at Kauksesauchung, seventeen miles to the west. These men were "from Susquehanna, very great river afar, and would likely be glad soon hear Jesus story." On July 24, Brainerd rode over "a hideous mountain" and for two days preached to the hunters. "We soon go home Susquehanna River," said the chief. "Come over for visit. Would like more talk."

Brainerd decided to make a special visit to the chief's village, Opelhaupung on the River, and so advised the SSPCK. "God seems to be opening a door for the spreading of the Gospel westward," he wrote. The Society replied, "Please undertake the visit to Opelhaupung as soon as possible." So Brainerd decided to ride to Opelhaupung, just about where modern Sunbury, Pennsylvania, is located.

FIRST TRIP

On the second day of October, 1744, Brainerd set out for the Susquehanna, accompanied by Moses Finda Fautaury; also two Indian chiefs from the Forks of the Delaware, and, his "dear Brother James Byram of Rockciticus." Rockciticus in the wilderness died in childhood; its very name has faded from the maps. But any who read William Milburn's fascinating *Rifle, Ax and Saddlebags,* will be aware that pre-Colonial heralds of the Cross rode into the wilderness along with the trappers and the traders. . . . "Byram is finely educated, surpassing me in piety and holiness," Brainerd confided to the *Memoirs.*

The westward journey was difficult: "scarce anything else but deep valleys and hideous rocks for sixty miles." Brainerd's mare broke a front leg among the boulders, so the Indians had to bludgeon the beast to death. *Brainerd completed the entire journey on foot!* They pressed forward through the cold Autumn mountains. In three days they came to Opelhaupung on the Susquehanna, a birch-bark village of twelve wigwams and about seventy souls.

For several days he preached for the Indian king, patiently answered his criticisms of Christianity, as based upon the vicious conduct of drunken traders. This was a hard criticism. Brainerd walked alone into the wilderness that night to plead with God for ministerial endowments.

*   *   *

"Would you like to have me return next Spring?" asked Brainerd as he was about to begin his return journey.

"Heartily willing," said the interpreter; "the king wishes his young people would learn."

At 4 A.M., October 9, the party arose, commended themselves

to God, and traveled with great steadiness until 6 P.M. "We made a shelter of barks. In the night the wolves howled around us; but God preserved us."

Brainerd made an entry on his return to the Forks of the Delaware, October 12: "Cannot but rejoice despite the hardships. Heathenish prejudices against the truth as it is in Jesus were in some measure removed. If that can be done, I am willing to spend and be spent in the service of the Susquehanna Indians."

* * *

April 18, in preparation for the second trip, Brainerd rode down to Philadelphia to interview the Governor of Pennsylvania, and urge him to secure permission for Brainerd to live on the Susquehanna.

"I'll be glad to do what I can," said the Governor. "The Six Nations claim the land. Only a few of them live there. The Indians there are a mongrel company of many tribes, and are vassals to the Six Nations."

* * *

SECOND TRIP

On May 7, 1745, Brainerd completed preparations for the second trip to the Susquehanna, "though he did not think, sick as he was, he could endure the journey again." But on May 8 he and Fautaury set out alone through "the hideous wilderness." A crackling, bone-chilling northeaster soon overtook them, and he was ready to perish. There was no shelter, no way to make a fire in the rain; their horses, buckeye-poisoned, were too sick to be ridden. Just at dusk the bedraggled pair found "an old bark" (tepee) in the wilderness.

On reaching the Susquehanna, Fautaury and Brainerd in the next two weeks traveled a hundred miles up and down the River; visited eight tribes. Brainerd, weary with the hardships, began

to tremble in every joint from the ague. There was such an evacuation of blood he feared he would perish. A trader who had neither proper physic nor food, gave him shack-hospitality for a week. Wan and sick, he continued his journey downstream.

The hopeless outlook of the second trip seemed typified in a particularly smelly old powwow, who was dressed from head to foot in animal skins, a boar-skin coat falling to his heels. Under a huge bearskin hat he had fastened a hideous painted mask, mouth awry. He came at Brainerd, dancing with all his might.

"I shrank back from him," wrote Brainerd, "though it was broad daylight. . . . Nevertheless some interest in religion appeared."

From Juncauta (modern Duncannon) he wearily rode homeward.

This second trip ran a total mileage of three hundred and forty. He found himself terribly depressed when he reached the Forks of the Delaware, May 30. He preached upon Isaiah 53:10: "Yet it pleased the Lord to bruise him."

* * *

THIRD TRIP

In August, 1745, as a result of his pilgrim-hermit vow, passionate longing again came upon him for the Susquehanna Indians. He decided to start back in September. But being apprehensive of the dangers and hardships, and, being also very ill, he asked the Indians at Crossweeksung to pray for him. He felt obliged to go. Had he not told God he would double his labor? The great revival was then in full power.

The Indian Christians cheerfully complied. . . . When he left them the September sun had still an hour and a half of shining. . . . They began to pray in their building, and continued until the break of day, never dreaming it was so late until they went out and saw the morning star.

*   *   *

September 9, 1745, he set out again, this time with a small party of six Indians. After three nights out of doors, he reached Shaumoking, now the modern coal town, Shamokin.

He was entertained in a big wigwam, but all night was sleepless by reason of a heathenish dance *in the house!* . . . Came again to a town they had visited before. Fifty big tepees sprawled out on both east and west banks of the Susquehanna and on an island between. Three tribes dwelt together—Delawares, Senakas, and Tutelas—an aggregation of three hundred, mostly drunken ruffians.

Too drunk, in fact, to listen to him! Just a very few appeared interested. He proceeded again to Juncauta Island, September 19, the party crossing the Susquehanna by canoes, swimming the horses. They came to the Island. Today one recognizes it as Juniata, right where Highway 11 crosses over the Juniata bridge.

There he assayed to preach to them, but it was to no effect. All night, about a hundred braves, having prepared ten fat deer, danced about a sacrificial fire. At times the flames, fat-fed, roared to prodigious heights. Their actions (he wrote in shocked surprise) were suited to raise the devil. The night of September 20, he walked to and fro in anguish, and at last crept into a little crib made for corn, and slept on the rails.

*   *   *

FOURTH TRIP

In the month of July, 1746, Brainerd again felt obliged to visit the Indians on the Susquehanna River. He was sustained by a hope of success arising from the continued revival in New

Jersey, and by the mounting interest at the Forks of the Delaware. The Susquehanna might now be favorable, if only he made
the trip! Physically, he felt unequal to crossing "the hideous
mountains" directly between the Delaware and the Susquehanna
Rivers. It would be wise to go by way of Philadelphia to the
head of the Chesapeake Bay, thence up the Susquehanna on the
low level route.

August 12 he set out, accompanied by six ardent New Jersey
Indian converts. . . . August 18 they reached Paxton (Paxtang) on the Susquehanna. His health was unmistakably bad.
During all of the next two nights he "coughed much bloody
matter." On the third night he lodged at Chambers' roadhouse,
and was much distressed by a crew of drunken whites. But
August 22, the party slept in the open with more peace of mind
than he found under Chambers' roof. . . . August 27 they arrived at Shaumoking.

He nearly choked in the thick smoke of a wigwam. A cold easterly
storm came the next day, so that he could neither remain indoors, nor
without, any length of time—pierced with raw air, or strangled with
smoke. As they proceeded, his clothing, despite the chill air, became
"wringing wet all night." September 1 he started for the Great Island,
fifty miles distant on the northwestern branch of the Susquehanna. September 2, having no ax, he climbed a young pine tree, and cut a few
branches with his knife to shield himself from night dews . . . exceeding
weakness now came upon him . . . he could scarcely ride . . . he began
to spit blood continuously. . . . September 3 he slept on a buffalo robe
. . . the next night he had no fire for cooking, for keeping warm, or for
frightening off wild beasts. . . .

By September 6 he felt he was a completely broken man. In all this
journey he had faithfully preached . . . now he had so little heart or life
he was ashamed of himself. . . .

The journey was over. He had proposed to tarry a considerable time
longer among the Indians upon the Susquehanna, but he must quit . . .
his extraordinary weakness, great nocturnal sweats, this coughing of blood
the whole journey.

The fourth Susquehanna journey was a dreadful series of exposures—alternate periods of heat and cold, rain and chill, as Fall and Summer fought for the mastery in the Pennsylvania wilderness.

He became so feeble and faint he doubted that he would ever reach home. . . . But he did. September 20, after two desperate sick spells, he came to Philadelphia. There he said to friends that he judged himself defeated—a failure. The Susquehanna had done for him. When he reached Cranberry, he found his poor Indians assembled in prayer service. They saw he had greatly failed. They sensed his end was near. He gave a brief account of his Susquehanna journey, was obliged to repair to his lodgings, and fell into a feverish sleep, saying over and over—

"I HAVE ENDURED MANY HARDSHIPS AND DISTRESSES, O GOD! BUT I WOULD GLADLY POUR OUT MY LIFE FOR THY KINGDOM."

*   *   *

This was already the case. He *had* poured out his life. He had nothing now to do but to die.

XXII

Equestrian Portrait

(AS OF AUGUST, 1746)

Near book end we are enabled to set forth what manner of man our Flagellant was. At first it seemed regrettable that we found him not before the evil days came. But afterward, we esteemed him as bearing upon him the print of the nails, far more than the unmarred lad of Haddam.

P

Then we *ourselves* traveled the River of Frustration. When we began the quest there was little of shadow: rivers reflected the sun! Then of a sudden clouds and darkness moved in, and we came to a placed named Sunbury . . . the coal towers melted away, the ancient village of Opelhaupung returned, and David rode into view. But—he was dying!

(Sketch Book)

WHEN A BIOGRAPHER SEEKS TO arrange his chapters in the most effective sequence, one of the difficult problems is, Where shall the full length portrait of the subject be located? That, of course, is tantamount to asking, At what time was the hero at his best, in his youth? in his maturity? in his old age? According to that canon, for example, the representation of Andrea del Sarto must appear prior to the age of thirty. Long before he was forty-five, his brushes had dried out, and there was mud in the eyes of his angels. . . . But an early-life portrait of George Bernard Shaw could have but little more than museum interest. The man never appears to have become lively before threescore and ten.

* * *

First thought, since Brainerd died before thirty, would be to sketch him as a junior collegian, when life is at its best. But at that interval we could never find him. To be sure, there were reports—

No one save a farm boy could ride the way he did, that substantial and practical horsemanship. He could—and no doubt did—steeple-chase over logs and gullies. He was a good specimen of that study so perennially refreshing—mounted youth. Good looking he was, medium height, lean of flank and jaw as a lad should be. Chin well rounded, thrust forward, a little up—quite becoming! If one is fond of reading such things as physiognomy and tea leaves, he would exclaim, "Ha! severe with himself, but indulgent with others."

Careful he was in appearance. His chartreuse trousers, snugly fitting his goodly legs, disappeared into the tops of high black boots. He had a long black coat, closed at the top about a frilly ruff, with buttons doubling in brass, then opening wide below the waist line to fall right and left of the saddle. He wore a jaunty Colonial billycock, with no brim to hide his dark, brooding eyes.

Bless me! that ancient description makes it sound as if the boy were on his way to Philadelphia to sign the Declaration of Independence!

*　　*　　*

But we never saw him thus. When Brainerd suddenly rode into view on the River of Frustration, my heart waxed heavy. I saw he was dying! No longer the carefree boy I dreamed. The furious devotion which earlier had lighted his face, now seamed it with furrows of care. He coughed a great deal, his body was distressingly thin, his cheeks sunken. Though young in years, the sun and the moon seemed darkened, and the clouds returned after the rain.

He rode in the manner of a man riding to get from one place to another, having no interest in either the horse or its gait. He appeared as fastidious as he did in student days; but there is a difference between old clothing carefully brushed, and the same garments student-new.

He is the same—but different. Voice is still high, but the morning ring has all but departed from it, and a little huskiness has appeared. Folks once thought his ways a bit too prissy: it did not sound good for a boy to talk about "affectionate melting in church services," or "meeting with sweet ministers," or "hoping that some dear creature might be saved." He still talks that way, but you no longer resent it. His travail has purchased for him the right to talk any way he pleases. . . . Once he was sensitive to profanity. He still is. *We* now wonder if we have not lost something by working up a callus against cursing. He is still "peevish and provoked by misdemeanor in church services." Now we sense that carelessness in such matters could be more culpable than indifference.

He is the same—but different. Once he seemed disfigured by an inflexible application—"never easy, under any circumstances, unless doing something for God. He never had time for small talk; all conversation must be profitable."

But today, though just as serious, he has become "remarkably sociable, pleasant and entertaining in his conversation . . . meek, modest, humble . . . far from stiffness or affectation in speech and behaviour. He seems to dislike such things." (Edwards, Summer of 1747.)

One can find in the *Memoirs* just where he began to put off the hard, unbecoming glaze of precocious piety—

He had been too severe in eliminating amusements: now he employs such diversions in living effectively to God. That is, he had lived long enough to find that deep-down piety took no injury from sunshine.

* * *

He is the same—but different. Once he was fired by "party spirit." Now, though he holds his views as tenaciously as ever, he has developed an excellent rule for steering a course in a world of conflicting religious views—

Through divine goodness, he has been enabled to mind his own business, and to let all men and all denominations alone as to their party notions; he preached only the plain and necessary truths of Christianity, neither inviting nor excluding from any meeting, any of any sort or persuasion whatever.

He is the same—but different. Once his lips were full and relaxed: now they are held in a firm line. Full lips could indicate a spirit ruled by casual or even whipped-up emotions; emotions summoned for a given task, then laid aside when the need is past.

Like the young dominie who found a proper pulpit ardor impossible unless he softly played "Hearts and Flowers" on the piano just before he went to the sacred desk.

Edwards' judgment influenced Brainerd to avoid such weaknesses—

The premium must be placed upon affections founded on light and judgment, rather than conceits or human whims. You have only to listen to a speaker a few minutes to discern whether he is powered by imaginary religion or spiritual discernment.

* * *

Well (our heart speaks), we did rejoice in the idea of Brainerd as a noble, though untempered youth, but this veteran of the Susquehanna is the one we select to remember. We admired the boy, but we love the warrior.

Young Mr. Brainerd, still winsome in the dew of his youth, must have been a pleasant person to contemplate. But this man of sorrows, who has broken his hands on hard realities; this horseman we found just before it was too late, is the Brainerd we cherish!

* * *

There he sat upon his steed, every inch a prince! Small wonder I knew not what to say to him by reason of admiration!

He bore upon his person the marks of his travail: those nights in the wilderness when darkness came down like ink. Sometimes he lost his way; every step was distressing as he rode over rocks, down hideous steeps, across swamps, extreme pain in his head, sickness in his stomach, not a star in sight. Sometimes, by the abundant grace of God, he came to a house; sometimes he lay out the whole night. One who did not approve of men like Brainerd, wrote: "He was personally indifferent to any hardships, utterly committed to God and to man. And that kind of man is entitled to our respect!" Ah, but such things have a way of breaking down the smooth mask of youth, engraving it with a maze of care lines, even before youth has departed!

* * *

And he bore upon his person the ineffable lights of his "permanent frames"! At first, he laid hold upon great convictions, and possessed them in his heart; then his great convictions laid hold upon him and possessed him body and soul!

Those who consorted with him at the last testified that it seemed as if the beauty of Another, whom he served and whose he was, mantled him from top to bottom. Even in his voice! As he talked, you suddenly became aware of the voice of Another.

Last night my soul was enlarged, and sweetly engaged in prayer that God would set up His kingdom in this place where the devil now reigns in a most eminent manner. I was enabled to ask this of God for His glory. . . . I was able to appeal to God with great freedom because it was His dear cause and not my own which engaged my heart. I appealed to God, "Honor Thy blessed Name and this is all I desire." O that the whole world would glorify Him! and love Him forever!

Packet 14

BRAINERD'S TOMB

Brainerd's life was associated with three picturesque American streams: the Delaware, the Susquehanna, and the Connecticut rivers. But it seems of more than ordinary interest that the Connecticut River should be the location of both his birthplace and his burial place. Of Haddam on the Connecticut, his birthplace, Chapter III carries the account. His tomb is located in the Bridge Street Cemetery at the eastern end of Northampton, not far from the Calvin Coolidge bridge over the Connecticut River. In the southeastern part of this thirty-acre cemetery there is a mound on which grow some tall pines, and near this mound are the memorial grave-table to David, lying east and west, and the marker for Jerusha. The tomb of 1949 is evidently a replacement of the one erected in 1747, which was "worn away with age and the spoilation of admiring visitors." Fortunately we are able to present pictures of both.

"The Northern Lights began to blaze in glory. I was delighted in contemplation on the glorious morning of the Resurrection." (From the *Memoirs*; see page 180, this book.)

The inscription on this early monument likely was carved directly on the
stone top. The text is quoted in Chapter XXIII. The text on the white marble
inset of the repaired monument seems to be about the same, save that the
death date is made to read "1747," instead of "1787." But the curious errors—
"died October 10" instead of "9" and the age "32," instead of "29"—are
retained.

A slab of red sandstone lies on the ground over the grave. A second piece
of red sandstone is upheld by five stone posts, four at the corners, one in the
center, about twenty-nine inches above the first. Both slabs are about
6′ 4″ x 3′ 3″. A piece of white marble about 23″ x 33″ has been set into the
top stone of the grave table. This bears the inscription. Next to Brainerd's
grave is Jerusha's, and adjacent to Jerusha's grave is a memorial monument
(cenotaphic) to Jonathan Edwards. Down Bridge Street, eastward, is the
Coolidge Bridge over the Connecticut River to Amherst, and across the River
is the Holyoke Range.

**BRAINERD'S
TOMB**

as of Easter
Sunday Morning
1949

*Photo by Miss
Cynthia S. Walsh,
of Northampton,
who also furnished
the description of
the tomb given
above.*

XXIII

The Long Ride Ends

(OCTOBER 9, 1747)

In which we are caused to remember the prayer of a certain ancient:

"Let me die the death of the righteous,
And let my last end be like his!"

"September 25, 1747. This day, I was unspeakably weak, and little better than speechless all day; however, I was able to write a little, and felt comfortable in some part of the day. O, it refreshed my soul, to think of former things, of desires to glorify God, and of the pleasures of living to Him! O, blessed God, I am speedily coming to Thee, I hope. Hasten the day, O Lord: if it be Thy blessed will, O come, Lord Jesus—come quickly. Amen."　　　　(Memoirs)

"This was the last time that ever Brainerd wrote in his own hand. The entries which followed, in a broken manner, were written by his brother Israel at David's dictation."　　　　(Edwards)

1718 - 1747

XANTHIC INTIMATIONS OF FALL, Winter—and Death suddenly appear both in Edwards' *Account* and Brainerd's *Memoirs*. The entry of September 20, 1746, which concluded Chapter XXI, brought the following memorandum from Edwards:

"Hitherto he kept a constant diary, giving an account of what passed from day to day, with very little interruption; but henceforth he was often brought so low, as either not to be capable of writing, or not able to recollect what passed in the day, or set down an orderly account. . . . His diary was not wholly neglected . . . but he had nothing now to do but to die."

Powerful presentiments of death came upon Brainerd as Autumn advanced. Frequently in the past, his mind had toyed with the idea of death; but this time it was different.

"I am now fully convinced of being really sick. . . . At other times I was perplexed with fears."

Yes, this time he was really sick. By dint of supreme effort only could he apply himself to the work of superintending at Cranberry—such as fence building. When he preached, he was sometimes seated; and sometimes after a few moments was obliged to stop. This made him feel brokenhearted; the end was coming, and he saw his people about to wander as sheep without a shepherd.

By November 3, he realized he was "utterly incapable." Perhaps much riding would help him; he would take a trip to New

England. He headed first for the house of Jonathan Dickinson, recently widowed, at Elizabethtown. He loved Mr. Dickinson. No wonder he was called "the safest man of his age."

But when Brainerd reached Elizabethtown, he became bed-ridden in Dickinson's manse for four and a half months. . . . Mid-March he was able to return to Cranberry.

He called his people together, and after having explained and sung a Psalm, he prayed with them. There was a considerable degree of affection among them. . . . Edwards wrote, "When he left Cranberry March 20, he little suspected he saw it and his beloved people for the last time."

Once again he headed for New England, the journey was several times broken by severe illness. . . . April 7 he officiated at the marriage of Jonathan Dickinson to his second wife, Mary Crane, in Newark—Dickinson being sixty-nine, she twenty-eight.* When the wedding party returned to Elizabethtown, David found his brother John waiting for him. John had been appointed supply missionary at Cranberry, during David's absence. David remained in the manse until his twenty-ninth birthday, April 20. April 21, he made his "final departure" from New Jersey. April 22 he spent his "final night" in New York City. When he left New York City, he would in less than five hundred miles of riding, pass through the gates of the City that hath foundations.

*   *   *

About May 1 he reached his home town, Haddam. . . . Two weeks of visiting among friends, particularly with his sister Spencer. He had often in his journeys visited in her home; she had been just like a mother to him. Little could he dream that in six weeks she would be dead!

* Exactly six months later, Dickinson died—two days before Brainerd's death.

May 27 he spent a dark night indeed at Long Meadow; death seemed to arch its sable wings above him. May 28 he reached Northampton, the home of Jonathan Edwards—and Jerusha! But in a few days he became restless. To remain in one place was difficult. . . . On June 9, Jerusha and he rode towards Boston. And if you know anything about *that route in June,* you cannot imagine anything lovelier. June 12 they arrived.

*   *   *

"Dear Mr. Joseph Bromfield, near Old South Church, desired to entertain the young couple in his spacious home." (Can you imagine a mansion on Milk Street?)

Ah, but those were delightful hours, so far as they could be, with him so ill. Boston's great and near great rode to Bromfield's to see the famous Mr. Brainerd. For a time, he was the Hub City's social lion.

A committee brought him the writings of "old Mr. Shepard," as David called him. Actually, the brilliant Thomas Shepard, pastor of the First Church, Cambridge, 1639-1649, was but forty-four when he died! But that was over a century earlier.

The committee, about to publish a Shepard manuscript, judged him turbid in places, and felt Mr. Brainerd "could clear him up where he lacked a word or two." This task Brainerd actually completed a few days before his death, adding a preface on his own for good measure!

The Commissioners of the Society in London for Propagating the Gospel in New England, sent a committee to Boston to interview Brainerd. They had great confidence in Mr. Brainerd's judgment. Would he suggest the names of two new appointees for mission work? This, too, Brainerd cared for before his death.

But the excitement and strain of the Boston visit proved too much. June 18, "the ulcers broke" (severe hemorrhage of the lungs). Obviously he was now doomed. Realizing this, David began to sign his letters, "your dying friend." One of these brought his brother Israel down from Yale at a gallop. It was at this time that David first heard, from Israel's lips, of Spencer's death, June 20.

The breakup of a family is always a melancholy affair. Father and mother were gone. Nehemiah was dead, Spencer was gone. Others of the nine were departed. In a short time he himself would be dead. Thank God! he would meet them in Heaven!

July 25, Israel returned to Yale, little dreaming that he himself was to die in January, 1748, at twenty-five.

*   *   *

On July 19, David was assisted—practically carried—into the services at Old South Church. He was greatly blessed with Pastor Joseph Sewall's "eloquent and spiritual discourse."

*   *   *

By the 20th of July, he felt strong enough to undertake the ninety-mile ride to Jerusha's home in Northampton. To avoid the sultry heat, they started in the cool of the afternoon. "Oh, Jerusha," he said as they rode slowly along, "you'll never know how grateful I am to get out of Boston! Funeral mourning is performed there with such pomp and outward show! I want my funeral quiet and simple."

*   *   *

In this portion of his *Account,* Edwards wrote his summary of "last times," one of the most pathetic passages in literature:

"David's last church service, the last time he prayed with the family, his last horseback ride, the last time he went out of our gates alive; his last messages—no others from his hand or at his dictation. . . ."

*   *   *

September 5, Brainerd was overjoyed—his brother John, "whom he loved dearer than all the world," unexpectedly came, riding up from Cranberry to Northampton. To complete David's delight, he found that John had brought with him a volume of his old writings—the account of The Solitary Place! This he read in tears; he was made to remember the mercies of God, which otherwise he might have forgotten. He asked Mr. Edwards to burn it. Instead, Edwards persuaded him to correct it, and make it available as biographical material; of which Chapters XVII and XIX of this volume carry a fuller account.

The next week John felt obliged to return to Cranberry—there was an epidemic among the Indians. "But I will return September 30."

September 17, Israel again returned to Northampton from Yale, the graduating exercises being completed, and remained with David until his death. After David made his final holographic entry in the *Memoirs* (see page 234), he dictated the remaining entries to Israel.

September 30 came—but John did not return, as promised. Edwards hints as to the keen disappointment of the dying man. . . . "Day after day passed—no John!" October 8, when poor David was past speaking, John came back! The epidemic at Cranberry had been critical. John had been obliged to remain with the sick and dying. "David seemed content with the explanation." That night he regained his speech, and for a long time visited with John.

"Brother," he said, "God has been good to me. He has answered my prayers. You are to succeed me at Cranberry. O Brother! live above the common rate of Christians; watch the movements of God's Spirit on your heart!—and if you must rejoice, rejoice in the perfections of God."

*　　*　　*

And now at book end, everything belonging to this story is sufficiently well accounted, save the most precious—Jerusha and David. For hours they visited in silence, "her face close to his." Edwards also reported that once David said to him, "It's like a little piece of Heaven to have her near me." Sometimes she wrote letters for him at his dictation. What collector today who would not pay a king's ransom for one of these letters in Jerusha's hand! Once, when she entered the room bearing a Bible for their daily reading, he said, "O that dear Book!"

*　　*　　*

One afternoon, early October, the dying man reached out and took Jerusha's hand. For a long time he had been trying to bring himself to offer an explanation. Up to this moment his lips had been sealed. He had never accounted for the flagellant vow he had made some months agone at Cranberry—the dark hour when he decided they must not marry—

"Farewell to the very dearest of all! I will spend my life to my latest moments in caves and dens, if the Kingdom of Christ may be thereby advanced."

The eyes of the dying lad were fixed upon the girl. How lovely she was! How wonderful, had it been possible to have made her his wife! But God knew—he had no liberty. Then, as if offering a final explanation, he said,

"O Jerusha! I could not have spent my life otherwise for the whole world!"

She understood! pressed his hand, tearfully put her face close to his. He added:

"Dear Jerusha, if I thought I should not see you and be happy with you in another world, I could not bear to part with you! ... But we shall spend a happy eternity together."

We think so too, and have no patience with crotchet-nursers who hold otherwise. We, too, have Scripture on that point!

* * *

Sunday, October 9, 1747, he passed over, with all the trumpets in Zion sounding. . . . February 14, 1748, four months later, Jerusha, too, passed over. For nineteen weary weeks this saintly girl had ministered unto her beloved, had contracted his malady.

Jonathan Edwards remembered how he had faithfully warned her, "Dear Child, it means death if you nurse David." He remembered too what she had said:

"Father, my place is with David, come what may."

He had known she would say that. He had wanted her to. She was just like her mother Sarah. But it broke his heart when she said it.

* * *

October 12, 1747, Edwards conducted Brainerd's funeral, using as his text II Corinthians 5:8. . . . February 16, 1748, Edwards preached another funeral sermon from the same text: "We are confident, I say, and willing rather to be absent from the body, and to be present with the Lord."

Jerusha was the dear child of his eleven. All the children were precious, from Sarah the eldest to Pierrepont the baby boy; but Jerusha he loved

Q

best. He would never forget how she got her name. He had been reading
about Uzziah's wife Jerusha, whose very name meant "Possession." So,
when for the second time Sarah travailed in pain, and a little girl came
to the Northampton manse—well, what better name than Jerusha? She
was "possession"!

(And if you, dear Reader, have a fancy for good calico names,
could you find a better, should a baby daughter come to your
home, than "Jerusha"?)

She was much the same spirit as David. She devoted herself to him—
looked on him as an eminent servant of Jesus Christ. She manifested a
heart uncommonly devoted to God, beyond any young woman he ever
knew. When she died she whispered to him, "O Father, I have desired
nothing but to live for God and His glory . . . and David said to me he
felt certain we would spend a happy eternity together."

The brokenhearted father held back his tears, and added, "I'm sure
David was right. Since Christians are to be forever present with the Lord,
shall they not, indeed, be present with each other?"

*   *   *

The Brainerd research brought to light an ancient Scottish
woodcut of his grave. Against a background of young pines "in
the old churchyard at Northampton, down by the bridge," there
is pictured a table-form monument, four marble pillars, each
about two feet high, supporting a slab of marble three by six feet.
Immediately adjacent in the illustration is a plain marble headstone upon which the name "Edwards" may be seen. "That must
be Jerusha's gravestone . . . some day I shall see it," I wrote in
the Sketch Book.

*   *   *

But that was not to be. Several years ago the Forbes Library
at Northampton purchased the fragments of an old magazine from
which even the name was missing. There was a brief article in

it concerning the graves. A transcript of the article is hereby printed—

* * *

"The old table monument bore this inscription—

Sacred
To the Memory of
the Revd. David Brainerd,
A faithful and laborious missionary
to the
Stockbridge, Delaware and Susquehanna
Tribes of Indians
Who died in this town
October 10, 1787
Aetat 32*

"The original slab was worn away with age, and the spoilation of admiring visitors. . . . Jonathan Edwards' daughter, Jerusha, to whom David was devoted, and to whom he was engaged to be married, died four months after his death, and lies buried close at his side."

* * *

The text upon Jerusha's headstone was—

Jerusha
Daughter of
Jonathan and Sarah Edwards
Born April 26, 1730
Died February 14, 1748
"I shall be satisfied when
I awake in Thy Likeness"

---

* Two items are incorrect. Brainerd died October 9, 1747, at the age of twenty-nine. The errors were likely made by the writer of the magazine article.

XXIV

Stirrup Cup

(AS OF JUNE 1, 1949)

He mounted the Pinto for his last ride over to the Santa Fe Station. We were certain it was his last ride—and so was he. He had such an appearance, together with that constant cough. . . . Our attempts at mirth were mirthless, and as tragic as they could be. One of the hands filled a gourd with spring water and handed it up to him—"Good bye, Jack! a stirrup cup!" Somebody among the boys sobbed outright. And Jack, like David of Bethlehem, poured the water on the ground—an offering to God.   *(Jack Highheels)*

"He will come, He will not tarry! I shall soon be in glory! I shall soon glorify God with the angels." (Last words of Brainerd.)

"And the great dragon was cast out, that old serpent, called the Devil, and Satan, which deceiveth the whole world . . . and they overcame him by the blood of the Lamb, and by the word of their testimony; and they loved not their lives unto the death." —*Revelation 12:9-11.*

* * *

Some one cavilled, "Of what importance were the life and labors of Brainerd? There were such small results!" Dr. S. Ralph Harlow, of Smith College, adequately answers that criticism in a letter to me dated June 7, 1949:

"I would call your attention to what I call 'the thin red line' of influence on the entire missionary movement here in America, from David Brainerd, through William Carey, the Andover Band, culminating in the Student Volunteer Movement, and the great missionary crusade of the past forty years."

*Y*OUR STORY COMES TO A CLOSE, Flock of the Pages. There is a sense of fulfillment; complete satisfaction for mind and heart, commingled with a tinge of sorrow. The flagellant pace always receives a full award from the treasures of God! Texts seem to sing as these last lines are set down: "He that loseth his life for my sake shall find it." Not only did Brainerd's self-effacement win the King's royal "Well done!" but, "he being dead yet speaketh."

Take the case of George Burlingame. He accepted a call to become pastor of a San Francisco church. Within a few days, April 18, 1906, the earthquake struck. All properties of the church were destroyed. Everyone expected Burlingame to withdraw his acceptance. But he didn't.

"Dr. Burlingame," I once inquired, as we walked the Redwoods of the Coast Range, *"Why* did you ever do a thing like that?" The dominie turned about. He seemed suddenly to resemble someone else. I know—he looked like David Brainerd!

"Well," he said slowly, "I couldn't forget the self-effacement of a certain Indian missionary."

*   *   *

The flagellant life is a repugnant thing to men who are at ease in Zion. But it does gain Joel's coveted theophany, "I will show wonders in Mount Zion!"

Many explanations have been offered which seek to account for Brainerd's exploits without giving credit to his "terrible de-

247

votion." Some of these, making him out to be a sort of white powwow, relay from one generation to another childish fairy tales of venomous snakes which refused to strike him. . . . Others try to assign his hiding of power to importunate praying. . . .

Not so! He overcame because he loved not his own life even unto death! He was the King's Perennial Flagellant!

*   *   *

In every age and clime, laborers who for His sake count not their lives dear unto themselves, invariably cry out in the end, "For my pains I have had double!"

*   *   *

We watched our beloved Flagellant ride back into the Susquehanna forests. . . . We turned Queen Elizabeth westwards. For many days agonizing questions have hammered upon consciousness—

Why couldn't David have had his Jerusha? Why did he always have to do things the hard way?

But the tires of Queen Elizabeth seemed to beat out an answer upon the tarred highway joints—

> "All through life I see a cross
> Where sons of God yield up their breath."

*   *   *

On this first day of June, 1949, that battle of fierce and shadowy forces is over. . . . Selfish protests are dead. The field is completely taken by the easy and blessed and natural law of Heaven—

> "There is no gain except by loss,
> No life except by death!"

Thank You, Neighbors!

ZEST IN THE COLLECTION OF DATA for this volume was maintained by the unfailing kindness and courtesy of the people whose help was sought. Before we ride on, we wish to thank you, Neighbors!

Mr. and Mrs. Egbert Wheeler Mersereau of San Jose, California, who generously shared the expenses incident to research, and whose enthusiasm for the Broad Brim Books has been "the author's reward" from the very beginning.

The Department of Rare Books, Princeton University, which through Howard Crosby Rice, Jr., present head, and Mrs. Marvin Dixon, former head, provided the microfilms of Brainerd's Hebrew Lexicon, Edwards' Northampton home, etc.

Yale University for valuable details in this book, some of which, together with the names of University officials who provided the same, are hereby listed:

Henry M. Fuller, Reference Librarian, Yale University Library, for a careful analysis of "the Brainerd manuscripts" in the Yale Library; and, for the photostat of page 1 of Brainerd's Diary.

Richard C. Lee, Director Yale University News Bureau, for the aerial view of the University; the photograph of the David Brainerd House, etc.

Joseph Setze, Assistant Curator American Art, Yale University Art Gallery, for the photographic reproduction of the portrait of Jonathan Edwards by Joseph Badger.

251

Elizabeth H. Barney, Registrar Yale University Divinity School, for precise information regarding the David Brainerd House in Yale's Sterling Divinity Quadrangle.

The Staff of the Forbes Memorial Library, Northampton, Massachusetts, for rare historic data; particularly the unfailing interest of Mrs. Hazel L. Damon.

The San Francisco Public Library, which through Laurence J. Clarke, City Librarian, placed at my disposal valuable reference books.

The Library of Congress, Washington, D. C., which enabled me to have available at Cedar-Palms rare references pertaining to Brainerd's life.

Two top-line American railroads, the Erie and the Lackawanna, for Delaware River photographs.

Mr. Milton Snow, Navaho Service, for a group of remarkable photographs of Indian life of the Painted Desert.

Miss Cynthia S. Walsh of Northampton, Massachusetts, whose painstaking investigations, hand-drawn maps, photographic studies and the like, have been indispensable. Miss Walsh is a type of all the good neighbors. When the question of remuneration arose, she wrote, "No charge! It has all been fun."

Mrs. Abbie E. Lange of the Northampton Historical Society for research, especially in connection with rare old prints.

Dr. S. Ralph Harlow, Department of Religion and Biblical Literature, Smith College, Northampton, Massachusetts, authority on the life of Brainerd. Dr. Harlow's care in reading this manuscript and his suggestions have been most valuable.

Kirk Brothers, Indian Traders, Gallup, New Mexico, for some of the Navaho photographs herein.

Dr. Harry W. Hansen, Pastor First Presbyterian Church, Medford, Oregon, for a rare Brainerd volume, priceless in the building of this one.

The Sunnyvale, California, Public Library for reference research.

Gilbert S. McClintock for permission to use certain prints from his book *Valley Views of Northeastern Pennsylvania* (published 1948, at Wilkes-Barre, Pennsylvania, by the Wyoming Historical and Geological Society).

And, Edith and Berlyn Stokely, of Gadtiahi, Oraibi, Arizona, "1949 Flagellants of the Painted Desert," whose insight into the mind of the American Indian through twenty-five years of labor among the Navahos has been most valuable.

* * *

Thank you, and others, not herein named. Thank you, indeed!

Deborah and R. E. D.